PERMANENTLY SUSPENDED

THE RISE AND FALL... AND RISE AGAIN OF RADIO'S MOST NOTORIOUS SHOCK JOCK

Anthony Cumia
@AnthonyCumia

This account has been permanently suspended

Twitter suspends accounts which violate the Twitter Rules

ANTHONY CUMIA
WITH JOHNNY RUSSO AND BRAD TRACKMAN

Post Hill PRESS

A POST HILL PRESS BOOK
ISBN: 978-1-64293-091-7
ISBN (eBook): 978-1-64293-092-4

Post Hill Press
New York • Nashville
posthillpress.com

Published in the United States of America

Dedication

To my mom, Rosemarie, with eternal love.

TABLE OF CONTENTS

FOREWORD

THIS BOOK IS LONG overdue. It marks the first time we are able to get a complete picture of Anthony's life, from his point of view, uninterrupted and without the self-imposed filter he spoke through for twenty years. Written accounts are, by nature, far less guarded than spoken ones. The author feels an obligation to give information, and then when rereading it during the edit, feels obligated to give a little more. Anthony has talked about writing a book for years, and now he has finally done it. About time, motherfucker. I cannot wait to read it, and not just because I am penning (typing) the foreword.

For the rest of my life, there will never be another phone call that shocks me more than the one I received in the spring of 2005. The *Opie and Anthony* show was finally back on the air after a twenty-six-month hiatus, after being canceled on terrestrial radio in August 2002. We returned on XM Satellite Radio in October 2004 and were fighting an uphill battle to return to the glory the show had experienced a couple of years earlier in afternoon drive time, and we knew it.

While we were on WNEW, the majority of my time was spent with Opie. We became very close friends, and he is the one who encouraged me to come back on the air time after time. It was also Opie who pushed to get me hired and who pushed to get me raises. Anthony was friendly and always fun on the air, but I got the impression he saw me as Opie's friend, so we were never that close off the air. We liked each other; we just never hung out. While we were off the air for two years and I was thinking of throwing myself out my twenty-second-floor window on a daily basis, Opie traveled the country with me as I did gigs and kept me updated on everything that was happening with our possible future.

About six months into our return, the dynamics between Opie and me began to change. He started fucking with me on the air and being a passive-aggressive dick off the air and between breaks. Not all the time, but it got to the point where my mother called me and asked what Opie's problem was. She had listened to the show and said he didn't sound like he liked me. I also heard that from other people, including some fellow comics who came on the show. What I now believe was happening was that he was uncomfortable or threatened by the on-air comedic chemistry Anthony and I had developed. The bullshit eventually got to a breaking point, and I was ready to quit the show. Six months in and I was seriously thinking of walking away. I began to dread going in every day.

Until that nondescript afternoon in the spring of 2005. I was at a Starbucks on 42nd Street with Bob Kelly and felt that familiar buzz in my front-left pocket. I looked at my phone. It was Anthony. I honestly think it was the first time he had ever called me. It occurred to me that I might be getting fired and was really tempted to let it go to voicemail. Before the phone was against my ear, he was talking: "Look, man, I just wanted you to know that you're doing great on the show. I see what's been going on and that you're getting discouraged. Well don't, because you're fucking hysterical and I can see he's been treating you like shit. I've had to deal with his shit for over twelve years, *and I fucking hate him!*"

He proceeded to unload and tell me about all the issues they'd had over the years, in particularly the way Op had treated his girlfriend, whom Anthony was still with. I was stunned. I thought Opie and Anthony were close friends, and this was after having been on the air with them for two years. I sat in the studio with them day in and day out and didn't realize they couldn't stand each other. What an unobservant asshole I had been. The relief I felt from that phone call is indescribable. I wasn't bombing on the show or close to getting fired. I wasn't crazy for feeling like something was wrong between Opie and me. I was doing well and contributing, and Ant was having fun with me on the air. From that moment forward, Anthony and I were silently bonded. So while I only joined the radio show because of Opie, I only stayed because of Ant.

Patrice O'Neal once said that Anthony could "access funny" faster than anyone he'd ever met. And while I'd never heard that term before, I knew exactly what he meant. Regardless of the discussion, the context, the topic, Ant has the ability to reach in with perfect timing and pull out something funny. He is by far the most talented radio performer I've ever known, and he's as fast as any comedian who has ever lived. I'm a great get if you need someone to describe an old lady falling down the steps or a blumpkin joke, but Anthony can be captivatingly funny describing air-conditioning duct installation. He can walk you through every aspect of the most monotonous activities, paint a perfectly clear picture, hilariously veer left and right, and will not once stray into the territory of boring. He has an incredible gift. For years I sat next to him completely awed by this, because I have zero ability to do it. I'm good at firing out lines, but I suck at giving interesting accounts. I've often said that if I escaped one of the towers on 9/11, I'd still lose people halfway through the story.

There is probably not another radio guy in history who has clicked better on air with comedians than Anthony. He is able to improv with all of us, on any level and at any speed we chose. Guys like Bill Burr, Louis CK, Bobby Kelly, Rich Vos, Colin Quinn, and of course Patrice would all tell you the same thing. When everyone was throwing insults around the room, you always knew that he would more than likely say something barbaric. But you also knew that nothing you would ever say to him would be off-limits. Nothing. If you were trying to be funny, you could pick up a sledgehammer and smash his fucking teeth out and he'd laugh. Anthony's complete lack of respect for the sanctity of any subject or institution is acceptable simply because he has a complete lack of respect for himself. That's not how I meant to say that; let me rephrase: Anthony puts the act or attempt of being funny above the idolatry of any subject, himself included.

For Ant, when it comes to being funny, everything in life we have experienced or will ever experience is piled into a bin. There is no order to anything and no hierarchy. On the air, where his mind works faster than that of any other person I have ever known, he isn't carefully examining each experience and maturely weighing the appropriateness of making fun of it. He is leaning way over into the bin with his ass up in the air, recklessly pulling things out, slicing them in half, and throwing them back in. All things in that bin truly are created equal. Nothing is allowed to be removed, nothing can claim offense, and there is no immunity. Murder and breast cancer live side by side with aluminum siding, *Dancing with the Stars*, crib death, Rocky Dennis, and modern jazz. Most importantly, that bin also contains his own divorce, deep insecurities, and the death of his father. Absolutely nothing is off-limits. He has no barriers on being funny, and he has never asked anyone to have them with him.

But let's not delude ourselves—hilarious jokes and thick skin aside, Anthony Cumia is a flawed human being. He is susceptible to fits of rage, drinks like Mickey Rourke in *Barfly*, and is currently in his seventeenth year of a midlife crisis. He's proven himself to be a terrible husband, a disgustingly loud neighbor, and an atrocious boyfriend. He is at times irrational and judgmental, and has the impulse control of a twelve-year-old. When feeling melancholy, most of us look at old photographs; Anthony does karaoke, singing Lionel Richie songs while cuddling a machine gun. He has said things that were sexist, racist, something-else-ist, and a hundred different things that were (fill in the blank)-aphobic. And despite having one of the most brilliant minds I've ever encountered, he will still resort to calling people "dickbags" and "fuckwads." He is most definitely flawed. But it's okay, a lot of comedic geniuses are. Robin Williams hanged himself, Lenny Bruce overdosed, Richard Pryor set himself on fire, Anthony Cumia gets drunk and goes on Twitter. Comedic brilliance is not automatically synonymous with good decision-making.

I can never overstate how incredibly lucky I was to work day in and day out for over ten years with this impulsive, hilarious savant. The night he was fired, I sat in my living room and cried, because I knew it was over. I knew that things would never be the same, and for the rest of my life, no one would ever be able to make me laugh so effortlessly on a daily basis. Ant is one of my closest friends to this day, and I see him as a brother. I've been blessed in my life to be associated with a tremendous number of truly funny people, and they've all made me laugh. But Anthony has made me laugh harder and more consistently than anyone else on earth. Even more importantly, he stopped me from making the biggest mistake of my life. When I was ready to walk away, Anthony picked up the phone on that nondescript afternoon in the spring of 2005 and pulled me back in. I'll never forget that moment, and I will always love him for it.

—Jim Norton, September 2017

PROLOGUE

THE CITY OF MANHATTAN has a population of roughly eight and a half million. That's a shitload of people. It's a mesh of international, relocating American residents and those who are actually born and bred right in the core of the Big Apple. Then you have the boroughs and, of course, the suburbanites like myself who consider themselves as much, if not more New York than the actual Manhattanites who get all the credit and props. I currently have a home on Long Island and an apartment in Manhattan. So fuck you! I'm a New Yorker any way you cut it and proud of it.

My experience when driving into NYC is almost like being in a transcendental state. I have a unique perspective when I'm just about to get into the city and I'm looking at that amazing skyline from afar. It's always been a time for me to reflect, dream, and curse out every asshole who doesn't know how to fucking merge into the Midtown Tunnel.

While working as an air-conditioning/heating employee, I would often drive in from Long Island in my beat-up company van. I would listen to Howard Stern all the time, and his show was the epitome of the greatest job in the world. Doing radio in NYC would be the best thing ever. I would imagine what it would be like to drive into the city to do that job. How cool it must be. On the job sites I would listen to him, and I wanted to be able to do that but surely wasn't moving in the right direction. I was doing nothing that was gonna get me there other than fantasizing about it. I vividly remember being fixated on that big stick coming off the top of the Empire State Building and knowing that's where everything was being broadcast out of. In the back of my mind, that's what I knew I was meant to do. It's always been easy for me to make people laugh. I had all the innate qualities to be the quintessential shock jock and zero idea how to make it happen. I didn't know how or if this was something that was obtainable or realistic. Back then I was making the trip to do a shit job that wasn't what I wanted to do. I just knew when I was making my way into Manhattan that I was destined for something bigger than driving that piece-of-shit work van and busting my balls doing manual labor.

I'm not sure if I believe in divine intervention or providence. Did I will my own prophecy of becoming a successful radio broadcaster into being? I have no idea. I do believe in luck, and I can tell you this with 100 percent of all my being: I never in a million years would have believed, when I was listening to Howard on my way into the city to do construction, that one day I would have people making their way into the city listening to me. I never would have believed that I would be writing this book. I'm very grateful. Hope you enjoy my story, but if you don't, there's no fucking refund.

CHAPTER 1

Back in the Day

ONE OF MY EARLIEST memories of childhood was hearing my father say, "Hey, Pissy Eyes, stop crying or I'll give you something to cry about."

I was always crying in my early years, mainly because I wanted to divert attention from what was usually my parents yelling at each other and my low tolerance for being a pussy.

There was constant turmoil and arguing in my household. My father, Joey, liked to drink, and he drank a lot. I was in a constant state of anxiety as a kid, which carried over to later in my life, as I ended up having horrific anxiety attacks in my teens and early twenties.

I literally never felt safe with my parents.

I was always thinking, "Oh, is this the moment we're all going to die?" And, "What's it going to be? Off a cliff? A car accident? A fire?" I was constantly in a state of fear, petrified that I could perish at any moment.

Dad would drive drunk, and it was terrifying. Red lights to me were my solace and a moment to go, "Ah, I'm still alive." Then the light would turn green again and I'd be right back to the terror of, "Holy shit, am I going to make it?"

When you speak about drinking and driving, it's normally about someone drinking and *then* driving. My dad would do the two simultaneously. He would drive with a beer between his legs and constantly be fiddling with the radio. He had a CB radio, and he'd be turning the wheel so the cord would get wrapped around the steering column as he would be trying to light one of his Tareyton cigarettes.

He may as well have been juggling knives and driving the car with his knees. I was horrified. That said, he never spilled a fucking drop and thankfully never crashed with me in the car.

He drove a Rambler, which was essentially a death trap on wheels. I'd be in the passenger seat with no seatbelt. If there was a seatbelt, it was shoved down so deep in the seat—along with the dry, fossilized McDonald's French fries and coins from the Confederacy—that I never would have found it. The dashboard was steel. There was no padding on it, and there certainly weren't airbags. I would have been dead if he'd hit a briar patch.

My father worked so hard at not working. That was the big issue between my parents. The fights were always about finances and my father's lack of income…and maybe a little cheating on the side.

The first job I remember my dad having was collecting the change from vending machines. I remember this period because there were nights I'd have Zagnut and Snickers bars for dinner. He'd also get gas and would just start pouring out quarters into the gas station attendant's hands; he was obviously pilfering from the machines he was collecting from. A vending machine once fell on his leg and then he was out on workers' comp. To this day, I think he purposely did it.

Dad had us moving all over the place when I was a kid. We were constantly packing up and moving from one location to the next, like a traveling horde of gypsies. If the Cumia family lived somewhere for two straight years, that was really something.

I was born in Flushing, Queens, New York, which I'd have zero recollection of if not for some home movies.

The first place I remember living was Long Island. The address was 8 Elwin Place. All the streets started with "El." There were Elwood, Elmont, and Elford, and I lived in Elford my kindergarten year. My dad tried to buy that house, and he had a mortgage. I guess that didn't pan out, because we eventually ended up in East Islip.

At this point in my life, I craved the spotlight, which applies to everything in my life, right up to and including this very moment. My entire job is based on me saying, "Look at me! Listen to me!" I don't remember a time in my life when I was not making people laugh and thinking it was the greatest fucking thing ever.

I would constantly be dragged by my parents to adult events, like a wedding, a christening, or whatever it was that Italian families did all together back then. There seemed to be a thousand people at these things, and afterward there were parties with food, drinking, and adults talking loudly.

Even back then, it was always, "Look at me!"

I would start doing impressions. At that time, I was watching movies on TV that had been made forty years before I was born, with people like Mae West, W. C. Fields, the Three Stooges, and the Marx Brothers.

I would do impressions of these people for adults, and they would laugh their asses off.

This would be like seeing a six-year-old today doing impressions from *The Godfather*. If I saw a kid doing Don Corleone or other *Godfather* impressions, I'd lose my shit.

I'm not sure my impressions were all that good, but just the context of them had to be outrageous. People loved it, and I loved making them laugh while being the center of attention. Making my friends or cousins laugh always came easily to me, but to make the grown-ups laugh was something else. It was more significant and more special. This was something my friends couldn't do.

This ability I had became a defense mechanism. I could usually diffuse any situation with a couple of jokes. I realized my asset of humor could help me socially with friends and, most important, with the girls. Laughter was a payment for me to get something, like: "I made you laugh, now I want something in return."

But sometimes my sense of humor got me into trouble I couldn't get out of.

OCT • 70

CHAPTER 2

Boomer

I WAS LIVING IN EAST Islip, Long Island, attending Timber Point Elementary School. Norman "Boomer" Esiason (who went on to become the NFL MVP in 1988 as the quarterback for the Cincinnati Bengals and is currently a broadcaster for television and radio) attended school with me in fifth grade.

Boomer was the gym teacher's pet, the very definition of "jock," and I was the complete opposite. I had zero interest in sports and couldn't have cared less if I did well in gym class.

Boomer was also the classic school bully; he could have been perfectly cast for any after-school TV special. He would walk around the cafeteria and fart in people's faces—literally walk up to someone, grab their head, lift his leg, and fart in their face. I knew his given name was Norman Esiason. Everyone knew this, but no one ever called him Norman.

If you called him Norman, he would beat the shit out of you. Not even the teachers would call him Norman. He was Boomer.

One day I thought it would be funny and I'd get a little jab in if I yelled "Norman" at him as I looked around the corner of the hallway without him seeing me. I saw him coming and yelled, "NOOOOORMAAAAAAAN!"

My friends and I had planned to just run off, but right as I turned around, one of Boomer's friends was standing in the hallway, and I knew I was busted.

He looked at me, smiling, and just nodded. Later that day, Boomer came up and gave me the obligatory "I'm gonna kick your ass after school!"

I was a string bean. I looked like a bulimic meth-head compared to Boomer, who was a jacked Nordic Viking in fifth grade.

The end of the day rolled around. It was springtime but still cold outside. I had one of those big snorkel jackets like Kenny on *South Park* wears, with a big tunnel hood. I decided I'd keep it on. Everyone usually rips their coat off and takes their shirt off when they fight. They're like, "Come on! Let's do this!"

I figured the more I had on, the less it would hurt. I didn't care about moving quickly, because I didn't know what I was supposed to do. I'd never been in a fight, and of course my first bout had to be with the Norwegian prince of East Islip.

We squared off in the school's back field. There was a big turnout. It's bad enough knowing you'll be getting your ass kicked, but hey, let's make it a school assembly for good measure.

I started circling around, because that's all I knew from the movies. I was moving my fists in this weird backward-and-forward rotation, like a punch-drunk 1920s boxer. Meanwhile, Boomer looked like a seasoned, undefeated heavyweight champ in his prime.

I knew this was a real fight and I had to throw a punch. I lunged forward and threw an overhand right, hitting him squarely in the forehead.

If you've ever seen Boomer Esiason's forehead, you know it's a billboard. It was always like that, even in the fifth grade. I felt my arm just tingle and go numb after the first blow, and I was paralyzed.

I got the first shot in with the hardest punch I could with my little straw arms. Imagine hitting one of those huge African water buffaloes in the head.

He felt nothing, didn't even flinch. Boomer then grabbed me by the coat, punching me once in the side of the head and once in the stomach. I was on the ground and it was over. Boomer had put on a clinic, like Tyson in a one-round fight. He walked away like this was just another day at the office…. "Ladies, come hither!"

I went home dejected and defeated, crying to my mom (Ro) that I had gotten beat up. I told her, "My arm doesn't feel right." She got the heating pad, which was the cure-all for everything. "Anthony, let me get the heating pad." "Mom, it's leukemia!"

The next morning my arm was like an overstuffed sausage. It was swollen, and I couldn't move my hand at all. My mom loaded me in the car and took me to Doctor Fuchs, who was this female German pediatrician straight out of Nazi Germany. She had the strongest accent, never cracked a smile, and sported a Hitler mustache. All kidding aside, she was always serious. "Your arm is broken. You broke the radius and ulna bones in your forearm."

I couldn't believe it. I had broken my arm punching this jerk-off's gargantuan head. I had a cast put on for eight weeks. It was embarrassing going back to school the next day: "Hey, everyone, in case you didn't hear, I got my ass kicked. Here's proof of it and a constant reminder."

You could see Boomer was very proud. He had the audacity to sign my cast. What was I going to do, tell him no so he could break the other fucking arm? I'd have been walking around with two casts. I should have asked him to sign it "Norman."

CHAPTER 3

This Is Gonna Hurt

IN MY EARLY DAYS, one aspect in which I resembled my father was never being able to finish something that I had started.

I saw a marionette on TV one afternoon and decided I was going to make one. I got some paper towels and tape and figured I'd try to make something out of them. I made a face with Magic Markers but failed to apply the most important part of the marionette: the strings and wooden pieces.

At this point, I was carrying this marionette around. My dad keenly observed this and quickly came to the conclusion that a marionette without strings was a fucking doll. He barked, "No son of my mine is going to be carrying a fucking doll around with him!"

I, of course, started crying and my dad said, "Hey, Pissy Eyes, don't be a faggot! I'm not taking you anywhere in public with you carrying that doll!"

Mom sprang to my defense:

"No, Joey, it's not a doll! It's a puppet!"

My dad retorted, "Until the puppet has strings, it's a fucking doll!"

My parents then started arguing about what qualified as a puppet, a marionette, and/or a doll.

Mom was very sympathetic to me. She was always sticking up for me whenever my dad was on the brink of a meltdown, which felt like always.

I rarely remember Dad relaxing. As a kid, I was in a constant fight-or-flight state.

Imagine, as a kid, constantly living on that edge.

"You want a knuckle sandwich, Anthony?"

Fight or flight.

Every day. Twenty-four hours a day. I guess it's what molded me into the upstanding human I am today.

My family had one reprieve a week, and that was when my parents would watch *Rowan & Martin's Laugh-In* on the tube.

Then I could exhale and decompress, because I knew that for one hour my folks would be consumed with this show. My brother, Joe, and I could hear our parents laughing together.

The show was on past our bedtime, but Joe and I would try to sneak a peek to see what was so funny. We didn't get the jokes but were fascinated by what was making our parents crack up. My dad would catch us and warn us to get back in our room or else.

He then would hang his belt on the handle of our bedroom door as a final warning. We'd see that belt buckle glimmering in the light, and we wanted no part of it.

The way my father handled things was like DEFCON levels one through five. A normal level one was a verbal threat to "knock it off in there." My dad would say, "Stop busting my chops!" I never understood that at first. I took it literally. I didn't know what "chops" meant.

One day I asked to borrow his power tools, and he said no. I kept begging him, and he finally said, "Don't bust my chops!"

I was like, "Okay." I thought he was giving me permission to use the power tools but telling me to just not damage the chops. I thought "chops" was his favorite tool.

The next DEFCON level for him was displaying his belt. This was what we were going to get if we didn't listen. My dad was a virtuoso with a belt. He knew how to use and swing it. He would fold it in half so it was doubled. He went with the straight-down-overhead technique, going right down the middle. He had a nice Reggie Jackson swing. It was terrifying, and getting hit with the belt was the worst possible thing to happen to me as a kid.

Whenever I got into trouble, I knew my dad was going to be dishing out the belt punishment. The hours I spent waiting for him to come home were punishment enough. I would freak out just at the prospect of getting hit.

My dad would essentially give me a spanking with the belt on the meaty part of my ass. He would talk as he hit with every syllable:

"Don't ev...er do that a...gain or..."

I was like, "No multi-syllable words, please! You're killing me, Pop!"

"I don't find this hu...mor...ous at all! The in...con...sis...ten...cies...in...your...stor...y don't add up!"

"Dad! Jesus! Call me an asshole, hit me, and let's call it a day."

My parents ended up separating when I was in fifth grade. At first, they tried to keep it from us by saying my father was busy working. I would see him once a week, mostly on the weekends. It actually made things a little better, because he seemed to be less angry and able to have more fun with us. There were the pre-pickup and post-drop-off times when my parents exchanged smirks and little verbal shots back and forth, and that was a little weird. That said, all the arguments finally stopped because he wasn't living there anymore, which was definitely a good thing. I did hate the fact that my parents were divorced, though.

When I was a child, my mindset was that I'd rather have the constant arguing than have to say my parents were separated. In hindsight it was obviously a much better situation.

Since my father wasn't around full time, my mom had to take over the role of disciplinarian, which didn't come easily to her. I think she wanted to show us that we couldn't do whatever we wanted. One time I got busted for lying about taking apart something just to see how it worked. I would disassemble something without ever being able to put it back together. I was only ten years old. I wasn't a fucking engineer. My mom saw the broken toaster oven in pieces and started the interrogation. She quickly surmised I was lying and was clearly the guilty party.

My mother, now forced into the position of enforcer for the first time, took out the belt my father had used so effectively, but she didn't know how to use it.

She grabbed it by the buckle but didn't fold it the way dear old dad had perfected.

So, if you can imagine this, Mom whipped the belt around like Indiana Jones and used an odd sidearm technique the way Randy Johnson would throw a fastball. I didn't know how to defend against it. My go-to defense was running into my bedroom and jumping in the lower bunk bed as far back as I could go. This worked well with my dad's overhead delivery because it was hard to get between the top and lower bunks. It took some steam off his trajectory.

Mom's first swat with the belt snapped out with the pointy part that was tapered and hit me directly on the head of my dick. I let out a scream so loud, it was comparable only to the screams of that little Vietnamese girl running down the street after she was napalmed. That's how loud and brutal my scream was. My mom instantly dropped the belt and started crying, asking me, "What's the matter?" She had never heard me cry like that before and knew I was really hurt. I said, "You hit my wee-wee!"

I now had to ice this deformed, inflamed, mushroom-like head of my cock. I had a Ron Jeremy head with a child's shaft. It looked like a doorknob. My mother never mentioned it and retired from ever disciplining me again.

To be fair, my mother made me feel safer than my father had. She always tried her best by pampering and caring for me. She was very sympathetic to my "pissy eyes." I was a needy, attention-whore kid.

My mother would consistently go on school field trips with me. Anytime our elementary school went to the planetarium or the museum, I asked if she'd be the field trip mom and she always said yes.

I would actually make wardrobe requests of her, like, "Mom, I need you to wear the red miniskirt and put in the pigtails." I made her dress up because my friends would always tell me, "Your mom is so pretty." I'd be like pimping my mom out for these field trips. "I want the go-go boots and the skirt that Dad says your ass looks good in."

All the kids loved my mom. She was the fun, nice mom. All my other friends' moms seemed old, and my mom was young, fun, and vibrant. One field trip we went to Radio City Music Hall to see *A Boy Named Charlie Brown*. My mom was super hungover, throwing up that morning and in pretty bad shape, but she promised she'd be the field trip mom. I remember her in the back of the bus chugging from a bottle of Pepto-Bismol. She was talking to all my friends with a pink tongue. The other field trip moms were looking at her like she was a degenerate. Hey, fuck them! She went, and it was a lot of fun.

During this period of separation, my father was dating different girls. Women gravitated to him, and he had a plethora of twenty-something bimbos. I'd be visiting my dad for the weekend and he'd take us to bars or his apartment.

Whomever he was dating that week would cook and make a pathetic attempt to be my mom. My dad had no self-control with women. He was never like, "Maybe I shouldn't? Ya know, this girl isn't all there; she's married and has a record." Perfect! It didn't fucking matter! If he found them attractive, it was going to happen.

My father was a lot like me, completely fixated on women; he tried to figure out how he could see every single one of them who showed any interest. My siblings and I went over to my dad's apartment one day, and he had this one girl cook us dinner. We just met her that once, and she wrote these little notes that she gave my dad to give to each of us. They were weird complimentary assessments of all the kids.

She mentioned Joe's talent for being a musician. My sister, Dawn, was so young that it was more or less about being a princess. Mine was that I was so funny, and she could see me being a comedian or an entertainment personality. Leave it to my dad to bang a clairvoyant. She was the Nostrad-amus of Mineola, and her mac and cheese wasn't too shabby either.

In all honesty, I don't know why it took my parents so long to tell us they were divorcing. But within a year, my father moved to California for a fresh start, living initially with his aunt in Laguna Beach and then in Dana Point. My father ended up moving to a predominantly equestrian Western-style town called San Juan Capistrano in Orange County, California,

which is where the swallows end up every year. He really made a complete transformation: buying horses, getting a cowboy hat with the boots, and drinking at the local Western bars.

Even though my father distanced himself from us geographically, he still stayed in touch with phone calls every week and an open invitation to visit him whenever we wanted.

My mother really stepped up raising us by herself. She could have easily denied us a lot of things and been bitter. She could have put herself first and us kids on the back burner, but Mom was very involved, kept us well fed, and made sure we had a great childhood. She usually worked three jobs at once, so she could make sure that my brother, sister, and I were well provided for. We never had to worry about anything, and she gave us the stability we needed.

CHAPTER 4

California

I WAS ELEVEN THE FIRST time I went out to California to visit my dad. He was living in a tiny apartment in Laguna Beach. It was my summer vacation from school, and Joe and I drove cross-country with Dad in his new Pinto.

My brother and I were in the back seat with a cooler full of beer between us. I'd just wake up not knowing where we were or what time it was, soaking wet from this cooler. It was like a NASA test and Joe and I were the chimps.

We drove straight through, stopping only once in South Dakota to shower and change. We saw sites like Mount Rushmore, which I viewed with one eye, half awake, and the Grand Canyon, which eventually led us to Dad's closet-size apartment in Cali.

Joe and I slept in sleeping bags on the floor, and most of our days on that vacation were spent in a bar. It was my introduction to shooting pool and throwing darts. Maybe it wasn't the most traditional family experience, but you take what you can get, and I still make money throwing darts to this day.

One memorable evening we took a trip to Tijuana, Mexico, which was cool to experience. When we came back across the border, the agents asked my dad if he was a US citizen, to which he replied, "*Sí, señor.*" Always the wiseass, my pops.

He was then taken out of the car and detained for at least a couple of hours. My dad always made things an adventure.

The next time I traveled to California, I was thirteen and went with my sister, Dawn. Dad was then living in San Juan Capistrano. He had a condo and a piece of property nearby, which we referred to as "the ranch."

Dawn and I decided to stay and live with my dad. I called Mom and told her we wanted to give it a shot living out there, and although she had every legal right to have us come home, I think she figured if we stayed in California long enough, we'd eventually come to our own decision to come back to her. It didn't take Dawn very long. She ended up going to our mom after a year, while I stayed.

I went to Marco Forster Middle School, and it was such a completely different experience from school back in New York. The aesthetics of the building were wild. The hallways were just roofs with posts and were wide open, because it was never freezing cold, and it certainly never snowed. The teachers had this groovy California vibe, and everyone was so nice, which was different from the New York "eat shit, fuck you" attitude I was accustomed to. There were definitely some assholes, but for the most part, everyone was laid-back and cool.

No Norman "Boomer" Esiason breaking my balls—or arm, for that matter.

I typically would walk a mile home from school directly to the ranch, and I'd see Dad and a Mexican named Chato Reyes. Chato and Juan, his brother, owned horses on the other side of the stable.

I'd get there, and they would have been drinking forty-ounce beers all day long. Mexicans had their own side, and the Americans had the other. The stables were segregated, which was strange because we were all friends regardless. They had thick accents and couldn't pronounce "jumbo," so they'd say to me, "Hey, why don't you get a yuuumbo?"

My first time drinking was at Jimmy Jackson's stable. This guy was a real nut whom everyone around town knew. There'd be a bunch of drunken men who would show up at Jimmy's to rope cattle and calves in a rodeo arena. There were no safety measures taken, and there wasn't anyone there to monitor what was going on.

Eventually it went from roping to riding the bulls. Jimmy welded together a rider chute like you'd see at a rodeo. These completely hammered cowboys would get on top of these bulls for usually three steps before getting thrown off onto their ass or head. Everyone would just start laughing. This was genuinely dangerous.

My dad asked me if I wanted to try it: "If you do it and stay on for at least eight seconds, I'll give you a Coors."

I replied, "Sure, Dad! Hell, if I survive this, maybe I can try playing Russian roulette?"

The prepping for the ride was the scariest part for me. They put a strap around the bull's midsection. That's what you hold on to. You'd have a glove coated in rosin, and you'd have to slip your hand under the strap. They'd pull the strap really tight, and then you'd have to grab and hold on to it. It's basically a slipknot tied around the bull—the theory being that once you let go, the slipknot would immediately relinquish you from your ride. This rarely worked. More often than not, these guys would get caught in this slipknot and dragged across the arena halfway hanging off the bull, held by nothing but their hand. Meanwhile, everyone else would be hysterically laughing at this poor bastard's expense.

I was truly worried that someone was going to die—particularly me!

I just wanted to be one of the guys. The idea of sitting around drinking a beer with them after riding a bull was something I needed and had to have.

The riding process goes like this: They put the bull into the chute that was made out of metal pipes. You have to sit on the bull. First you need to stand on these metal pipes so you're above the bull and gently mount it. You don't want to startle the bull in the pen. Then a guy makes sure that the slipknot is pulled tight in your hand. The last thing they do before they open the chute is pull a strap that goes around the bull's balls, which makes it instantly start kicking. If that isn't enough, they hit him with a cattle prod on the ass. Imagine, if you will, someone squeezing your balls in a slipknot and simultaneously zapping your ass while riding on your back! You're going to want to get that person off you immediately.

So I was on the bull and they released it from the chute. This bull was bucking, kicking, and spinning in the air ferociously. I felt like I was on for the eight seconds. In reality, I was thrown off as soon as the chute opened. I was on for literally a mere second. I turned and looked at the chute, and it had to be a foot behind me. I didn't travel very far. Everyone was laughing but also yelling, "Get out! Get out of the arena!" This bull quickly turned around looking for payback for being wrongfully Tasered and having his balls crushed. Can't say I blame him.

I was on my hands and knees scrambling back and was able to jump through the fence to safety. I made it unscathed. My father came over and popped a cold Coors for me. I drank a beer with the guys after riding a bull. To this day, it's one of those defining moments that signified the transition between me as the kid who used to play with toys and the young man who was now hanging out socially with adults. The fear of riding the bull was inconsequential compared to drinking a beer in that circle of men discussing the short-lived ride of my life. I was finally one of the guys, and it was great.

I made friends with Richard Szczepanski, who also hung out at the ranch. Richard was two years younger than I was and became my best friend. He was good-looking and the girls absolutely loved him. They wouldn't leave this guy alone. He was young and showed no interest in these chicks who were practically throwing themselves at him. I was like, "Please help me out here! At least put some effort in, so I can get some of your fall-off broads. You're chasing these girls off, for Christ's sake."

At this point my dad and his girlfriend, Corey, noticed I was spending a little too much time in the bathroom. I was now officially a teenager, being the ripe age of thirteen. My dad wanted to make sure I had the proper experience.

During this time, there was a nineteen-year-old girl I knew from the stables, Christine, who had the nickname "Buzz," because she was always buzzed drinking.

Christine was very flirtatious and always shaking her ass and showing off her gigantic breasts. She was ready to go, and my dad knew she was a suitable candidate for his son's first roll in the hay.

One night my dad and Corey were going out and I was staying home by myself. Buzz was already at my house and said to my dad that she was going to stay with me and hang out. He was like, "Okay, take it easy."

So then I was alone with Buzz, and we'd been by ourselves before and watched comedies like Monty Python together. I had been at the ranch that day riding horses and was filthy, so Buzz suggested I go upstairs and take a shower. I didn't even think twice about it and just did it. I got done with my shower and was drying off and walking toward my bedroom when I heard Buzz in my dad's room call out, "Hey, what are you doing?"

I was like, "What?"

I walked over to the bedroom doorway, and there was Buzz in the bed with the covers pulled up just to her belly button, with these huge, amazing tits staring at me. She seductively tapped the bed and said, "You want to come on in?"

Oh fuck yeah, I wanted to come in…and out…and everywhere else I could come other than by my hand in my sock.

Mind you, these were the first real tits I ever saw, and I instantaneously realized that I was going to get to see what was under the blanket too. This was Halloween, Christmas, and my birthday all rolled into one.

I jumped right into the bed, and she started touching me and grabbing my cock and said, "Can you take your underwear off?"

"YES! Yes, I can and yes, I will! Whatever you want, I will do!"

She did everything you could imagine to me. I came fast and hard, like a thirteen-year-old virgin should. Right on cue. I was now officially a man; getting laid for the first time was life-changing, and I seriously looked at things differently. I was like, "Now I get it," and by "it" I mean life. This was what everything we do was all about.

Everything a man strives for, whether it's money, materialistic things, or self-worth, is for sex. It's what secretly drives every man. Buzz and I continued to exchange bodily fluids until the day I went back to New York. It wasn't a boyfriend-girlfriend relationship; we just did it when the opportunity presented itself. I still played with my model rockets and hung out with kids my own age who didn't have a clue what sex was all about. My friends were talking about things like, "I have peanut butter and jelly, and I wanted ham and turkey."

I was thinking, "You don't have a clue what life is about, do you? Why are you talking about a sandwich? It's about a penis in a vagina."

Buzz was great because it was just sex. I was at that age when I wanted girls to like me and actually go on dates. I wanted a girlfriend and couldn't do that with her.

Back in 1975 we didn't have social media. I want to smack kids in the head these days for how easy they have it getting laid or even seeing nudity, for that matter. Back then, seeing nudity was amazing. The closest thing we had to social media was citizens band radio, otherwise known as CB radio. Every trucker had one, and back in the mid-seventies it was the rage. It started with truckers and eventually made its way into regular cars and homes as well.

My handle was the Wrangler, because I wrangled livestock. We had a base station at our house, and I thought this would be a great way to meet people. One night I heard a girl who went by the name of Dream Weaver. Instantly my imagination started going. I was attracted to her voice. She sounded sweet, and I really wanted to start talking to her.

I reached out and said, "Hey, Dream Weaver, this is the Wrangler. Ya got your ears on?" She got back to me, and we started talking for about a week or so every night on the CB.

I spoke to her about my horses and school. She told me about her school and herself. We were about the same age. She too was into horses.

I finally worked up the nerve to ask her out on the CB and set up a date. She accepted. I started planning immediately. I had a week to prepare for this weekend date. My plan was to meet Dream Weaver early Saturday on my horse. I would bring another horse with me so we could both ride into the hills, and I would be armed with my rifle and supplies in the saddlebags.

My goal was to camp in the hills from Saturday night into Sunday morning. I was going to hunt down a rabbit. I knew how to hunt, clean, and cook a rabbit. I was of course sharing the details of my fantasy date with her on the CB leading up to our finally meeting up in person.

I was completely caught up in this fantasy and envisioning her as my girlfriend. Saturday morning came, and I had never tended to the horses so well. I made sure they were clean, and I even washed the saddles with saddle soap. I went all out!

I packed my saddlebags, including a few beers—thinking ahead to get her loosened up a bit. I didn't leave any detail unattended. I was ready for my dream to become a reality. I took my horse and towed her horse by wrapping the reins around the old saddle horn.

Our meeting destination was the riverbed where two rivers met and led into the San Juan River, which led to the beach. I got there early and sat on my horse waiting. Way down the river, I saw a semblance of a figure making its way towards me. My adrenaline started going and it dawned on me, "This is Dream Weaver! My fantasy is finally coming true." She started getting a little closer and I noticed the proportions of this girl's figure, and they weren't good.

She was now getting closer and I was thinking, "Oh please, God, don't let this be her," at which point her arm went up in a big, enthusiastic wave. My entire weeklong fantasy I had been building up in my head was crumbling apart. When I saw this mammoth girl, I surmised a rabbit wouldn't suffice. I was gonna need to bag a moose to feed this one. The closer she got, the bigger she got.

Mind you, look at how things don't fucking change. CB radio was our social media in 1975. In 2018 you can still get tricked by photos! Nobody ever looks as good. There's always a guise. Don't forget, even if you find someone who looks exactly as good or better than her picture, she's probably still wearing makeup!

We were now face-to-face, and I was so disillusioned and visibly disappointed that I could barely hide it. Dream Weaver was very excited and just gushing with her introductory greetings: "Hi! Oh my God! How are you?"

I mustered up, "Okay, get on." At which point the horse gave me a nasty look. He was like, "Really?"

She got on and we rode up into the hills. She did not shut the fuck up. At this point I was disinterested. If she had been hot or at least cute, I'd have listened to her babble all day. I'd give her the "Oh yeah! I know exactly what you mean. Yes! You're so funny!" At this point with Dream Weaver, I was literally mumbling to myself, "Just please shut the fuck up." I was looking at my watch, and it was moving as slowly as the horse Dream Weaver was riding. Time was standing still. I wanted this date to be over. No camping, shooting rabbits, drinking beer, or combining our sleeping bags. I would have needed eight sleeping bags for her to fit.

About two hours later I said, "We've gotta go. I told my dad I'd have the horses back." I think at that point she understood. She said okay and she became quiet, and we made our way down the mountain in silence. She made the trip with me back to the ranch, and I put the horses away. I think I shook her hand goodbye like we had closed a business deal.

I saw Dream Weaver one more time. She was sitting around a campfire at one of the other stables about a month or two later. She was singing songs with some of her friends from school, who were all incredibly hot! I couldn't have gotten one of the hot ones? I would have fantasized shooting a rabbit for every one of them. But I had to get fucking Dream Weaver! We saw each other, and both of us gave a very quick tip of the head. We never spoke again. It was a great lesson to not get so caught up in what you think something's going to end up being.

Fast-forward a couple of years: Richard and I were having a sleepover in a treehouse located at the ranch. We were drinking and ready to cash it in for the night. I had just finished my beer and was lying down ready to go to sleep, when I heard Richard whisper to me:

"Anthony, can I suck your cock?"

I swear, I couldn't believe what I was hearing, and once again, I heard Richard whisper to me:

"Anthony, can I suck your cock?"

My nose was pressed against the plywood of this badly built tree-house, and I just pretended that I was sleeping and ignored him. I woke up the next morning and never said anything to him. Needless to say, that definitely changed our friendship, and Richard started hanging out with other kids who were more flamboyant.

Joe came out to live with us in California, because he was getting into drugs and getting to be too much for my mom to handle. He used to hide his joints in my model rockets, and one day I decided I was going to try one and see what it was all about. I had heard you don't get high your first time anyway.

I took a joint and went by myself to the riverbed, and there was a pump house, which was an old tin shack that was unlocked. It was pitch dark in there, and I went in and smoked the whole joint. I was sitting and wasn't feeling anything, but I couldn't see anything either. I got up and opened the door, and can equate the experience only to *The Wizard of Oz* when Dorothy goes from being in black and white to entering Oz and it's in color. That's exactly how it felt. I went from "I don't think this affected me" to "Oh my God, I am so fucking stoned."

Once again, I had hit another crossroads moment in life when I was like, "I think I'm going to be smoking this shit."

After the school year finished, it was time to head back to New York.

That trip back from California was a nightmare…and that's being polite.

I was with Joe, and we were just supposed to be visiting our mom for summer break. She sent my father American Airlines tickets for the two of us.

Well, my father saw the opportunity to make some money by cashing in those tickets for a full refund and then putting us on a Greyhound bus from LA to NYC.

I know, "Father of the Year" written all over him.

Instead of a simple five-hour flight, we had now embarked upon a week-and-a half journey with only fifty dollars between the two of us. It's not like I was this brave kid who relished the opportunity to travel on a bus cross-country and bond with his brother.

I was a nervous, paranoid, petrified sixteen-year-old, thinking there were murderers and child rapists lurking about on this bus. I looked at everybody with a stink eye as a potential suspect.

The people getting on this bus from Los Angeles were just a cavalcade of freaks and degenerates. There was a Greek bum who came on with a huge bottle of ouzo. He was hammered the whole time. There was a female prostitute who was brought to the bus by a guy who looked identical to the pimp Huggy Bear on *Starsky & Hutch*. She was white but spoke as if she had been raised speaking Ebonics.

She kept yelling out the window, "Oh Antoine! You be a fool! Stop tripping, baby! You crazy, Antoine!"

He was sending her to Chicago to open another franchise there for whores.

Then there was a lovely, sweet girl who came on board who was traveling to Cheyenne, Wyoming. The rest were just transients who got off in each city while others got on. Now, I realize that in the mid-seventies things were cheaper, but my dad had given us only fifty dollars for a week and a half. Was he out of his fucking mind? When we got to Las Vegas, we took the little money we had left and tried to make some more on the slot machines. We wound up losing just about everything and found ourselves completely broke and starving from Las Vegas to NYC.

The normal way to go about something like this is to do shorter trips. You would break it up by getting a hotel to sleep and shower in. Not us; we were sleeping on the bus and not stopping till we got to our destination. We made friends with the prostitute and the girl going to Cheyenne. We stole the ouzo bum's bottle and started drinking from it to keep ourselves occupied.

We all were drunk, and my brother started making out with the Wyoming girl, and I tried to negotiate a payment plan with the prostitute for a hand job. It was just the strangest journey with the strangest people. It was frightening and desperate. I was constantly starving.

The bus would stop to refuel, and my brother and I would look for bottles to recycle. We tried to scare up enough money to buy a sandwich or just bread. We finally got to Cheyenne, and this girl and my brother were so chummy by then that she decided to stay on the bus the whole way to NYC. Most guys can't even get a girl to go for a beer run, and Joe had this broad going an extra seventeen hundred miles. That ouzo was the shit.

This girl had some money, which fortunately she shared with us, and a week and a half later we finally fucking made it to the Port Authority bus terminal on 42nd Street. I don't think we had even stepped off the bus when a cop grabbed us and said, "Come on. You're coming with me!"

The cop obviously thought we were runaways. He took us to his office and asked us, "Where are you coming from?"

We told him, "Los Angeles!" and how our dad had sent us to visit our mom for the summer. The cop was like, "Really? You're not coming here to make it big? To do something? What are you boys really doing here?"

My brother had a knife, and the cop asked him why he had that. Joe explained that where we were living it was common for guys to carry one. The cop asked, "Where's your bags?"

We told him they were still on the bus. He said he wanted to see our bags, and I had to stay while Joe retrieved the bags.

Meanwhile, it had dawned on me that Joe had brought back a bunch of Thai stick weed. Yes, living with my father had really helped straighten Joe out—not. If anything, I think he became savvier and better educated, with a better product. I was thinking there was a chance Joe wasn't coming back, or he was going to get us popped. I just wanted to get back to my mom's and eat some capicola for Christ's sake.

When my brother went to get the bags, I was held as collateral until his return. I don't know how he did it, but he got the girl from Wyoming to claim Joe's bag was hers, and she had the bag with the weed in it. Joe brought back my bag, and we were in the clear.

The cop said he needed to call my mom. My mother was worried like a basket case the whole time and livid that my father had put us in this situation. We had to call her constantly. I told the officer that my mom was really nervous, and he should please lead off the call with, "I have your boys here and they're okay." I said, "Please do that," and he was like, "Yeah, okay, whatever."

He called and my mom answered. "Mrs. Cumia? This is Lieutenant [such and such] from the Port Authority NYPD. Do you have sons named Anthony and Joe?"

I yelled in the background, "We're fine!"

The way he was sounding, the next words out of his mouth were going to be, "We have your sons in the morgue, and we're gonna need you to come down and identify their bodies."

We finally got everything cleared and got on a train to Huntington, New York. My mom was there waiting in her car and said, "I've never smelled anything worse than you two." We hadn't showered in a week in a half, we had been drinking ouzo from a bum who had been sweating alcohol, and we were practically eating out of the garbage to stay alive. That girl went straight back to Cheyenne, and we never saw or heard from her again. Shocker, I know. I called my dad later that day to tell him we had finally made it and that he owed me ten bucks for the hand job I'd gotten from that hooker.

To which he replied, "Hey, I told you, you'd like the bus!"

CHAPTER 5

Back for Bad

W HEN WE WERE FINALLY back in New York to visit Mom and other relatives during that summer break, I decided I wanted to stay. I realized this was what family was supposed to be like.

Looking back, I'm glad I had that experience living with my father in California. He went from being an overbearing, scary dad when he was living with Mom to a guy whom I finally got to understand and ultimately like.

Living in California with my dad was divine intervention, and it definitely helped shape a big part of who I am today.

So I went from the laid-back West Coast vibe to a very structured high school in New York that had bigger expectations. I was supposed to be in certain places, to achieve more academically, and I started out the year saying, "I'm going to crush this."

Then by the second week, I was like, "I hope summer school has air conditioning."

I realized I just didn't care for the mandatory structured curriculum. If I was interested in a subject, I'd get an A, and if I wasn't, I'd get an F. There was no middle ground.

Hell, I was an exotic being from California. It gave me a more developed perspective than a lot of my friends.

My high school years in New York were all about getting high and laid. I had pussy on my mind 24/7. The whole "bros before hos" thing did not apply as far as I was concerned. I was the worst when it came to girls and my guy friends.

I took a girlfriend from one of my friends, Frank, and made her my girlfriend. It was terrible, and I just didn't give a shit. It was almost this primitive territorial thing that I just wanted all the girls to myself. One of my best friends, Joe Currie, used to say, "Ant, you're a fucking weasel!"

I would see him talking to a girl across the room and go out of my way to start telling jokes and try to cockblock him. I wanted the attention of every single girl in the room. I'm lucky I had great friends who didn't just beat the shit out of me, because I definitely deserved it.

I ended up quitting high school. I know it's a little disappointing, in retrospect. It's not like they have GED reunions. In eleventh grade, the dean of my school called me in and said, "There's no way you're going to pass this year, Cumia. Why not try taking the rest of this year off and see what it's like getting a job full time? Then come back next year after you see what it's like in the real world. Maybe this will give you more drive."

I was thinking, "You're giving me permission not to come to school?"

I left in my junior year and started working, washing dishes at Chicago Pizza & Pub. I also worked at an electronics place called Deutsch Relays. It sucked working at these places, but I loved having money. When the weekends came around, I would still hang out with my friends from school, and I was the only one making it rain with the "dough-ray-me."

Eventually, I did go back to school, but it didn't last very long. The dean's advice backfired, because I started getting a taste of making money and resented not making any while I was back in school. So I ended up quitting my second attempt at eleventh grade.

Leaving school didn't stop me from educating myself on subjects that I wanted to learn about. I was fascinated by space, space travel, and astronomy. I would go to the library and find really terrific books and read them. I didn't need a teacher to tell me what and when I should be learning.

That lasted a couple of years until my mom finally decided she had done her job and it was time for me to move out. She gave me a move-out date by instructing me to get my affairs together and start looking for a place to live. I've had landlords more sensitive than my own mother. She really wanted me the fuck out. She was marking off the days on the calendar.

I didn't do anything to properly prepare for this. I didn't have anywhere to go. I went to different friends' houses and crashed on their sofas. I had no ambition to do anything other than party and get by day to day.

If someone gave me a couch to sleep on, I'd stay on that couch until the person told me to leave. In 1984 I stayed with my friend Dave Ciemielewski and his family, which included his two brothers, sister, and mother, who was an invalid and partially paralyzed.

Mrs. C said I had to do stuff around the house to earn my keep. I was the houseboy, and I fucking loved it!

Everyone would get up early for school or work, and it would be just me and Mrs. C left in the house. I would vacuum, dust, clean the dishes, shop for food, and keep her company watching *General Hospital*. She'd be in her in Craftmatic adjustable bed, and I'd be in a chair next to her smoking cigarettes, hoping for the reunion of Luke and Laura. Hey, I'll admit it, I was always looking forward to the next episode.

One time during the first couple of weeks I was staying there, I was sleeping on the couch and could hear Mrs. C hobbling towards me. She could kind of walk with a limp. Through one eye

I saw her walk over to the fireplace and grab the fire poker. She walked straight at me with the poker, and I was thinking, "What the fuck is she doing?" And, more important, how was I going to explain beating the shit out of a half-paralyzed woman who was my friend's mom?

She stood over me with the fire poker in her hands with the point facing right at me. I thought, "Hey, if you want me to leave, just say so; you don't have to kill me." I decided that if I saw the poker start moving down, I was going to have to grab it and beat her head open with it.

Mrs. C then just put the poker away and went back to bed. I was beyond creeped the fuck out. I woke up and went about my business that day, but during dinner that night with the family there I said, "I have to bring something up. Early this morning, I know I wasn't dreaming, I saw you, Mrs. C, come up to me and raise a fire poker right above my head like you were going to stab me with it." She started laughing hysterically to the point where I thought she was going to choke.

Well, her son's room was directly above where I slept, and Mrs. C couldn't walk up the stairs. So apparently, every morning, while I was normally in a deep sleep, she would wake him up by banging the fire poker on the ceiling. She said some mornings she contemplated using the fire poker in my pants. "Oh, Mrs. C!"

I stayed with them till they moved.

I then got a place with Sean Ciemielewski, who was the middle brother, and my girlfriend at the time, Carrie. We rented the downstairs of a house in Greenlawn, Long Island. This was a fucking party house. We never paid rent even though the landlord was constantly trying to shake us down for it. My brother ended up staying there for a little while too and sold coke out of the house.

We'd have people banging on the door at all hours of the mornings with stereos, shit stolen from their relatives and, in a perfect world, cash to purchase blow from my brother. He didn't stay with us too long. Sean, Carrie, and I did live there for a good four years. This was the crash pads of crash pads. There was a pyramid of beer cans and dirty dishes stacked

to the ceiling. It was the house that people came to hang out and get fucked up in. Carrie was technically my girlfriend, but we didn't have any real love connection. She was like one of the guys. She was there because she could put up with the shit guys do and say when they get together and drink.

Then Sean moved out, and Carrie and I needed to find another place. We ended up moving right around the corner into Carrie's cousin's house. We lived there almost a year until I met Jennifer, who would eventually end up being the biggest mistake of my life. I mean my wife.

Jennifer was a bartender in Greenlawn. What were the chances of my falling for a girl who poured drinks professionally? As it turned out, pretty fucking good.

Jennifer had a great body and was twenty-three. She was everything you like about a girl before you're in a relationship with her. It was 1989 when we hooked up, and at this point, Carrie and I had zero chemistry sexually. She just wasn't into it. It seemed more like a chore for her.

Jennifer could be considered sexually adventurous. The first time we had intercourse, I had to come home to Carrie and I had the smells of passion all over me: sweat, cum, vaginal juices, and spit along with a spritz of disloyalty. I knew that if Carrie saw me, she would smell that I'd just had sex. I was driving a Baja Bug at the time, which was having engine problems. I decided to pour gasoline on myself and reach underneath the car to get oil and grit all over me to mask my infidelity. I got home and said, "Son of a bitch! This car broke down again! I finally got it started. Don't even get near me; I'm a mess." I was just going to jump in the shower and wash off the gas, oil, and vagina.

It would take me many years to realize it was going to take a lot more than gas and oil to clean the stink off Jennifer's and my marriage.

CHAPTER 6

My Shot

IT WAS 1991 WHEN Jennifer and I said "I do." It was an unforgettable year, because I also turned thirty, which was the reason I got married in the first place. I felt it was time I had to do something with my life.

My mom was working at a bar in Commack, Long Island, about an hour outside Manhattan. I knew all her customers, and when I went in there they'd always go, "Hey, Ro, get your kid a drink." This was a common occurrence from the time I was of legal drinking age up until the time I hit the big three-oh.

For some reason when I hit thirty it dawned on me, "When am I not gonna be Ro's kid? I gotta do something to be an adult. So I'll get married!" Isn't that a great reason to get married, because you feel like you're supposed to by a certain age? I just didn't want to be thought of as a kid. It was all in my head and ironically, in hindsight, it never stopped. To this day, I still consider myself exactly as I was then. I've just accepted the fact that I'm in a constant state of arrested development. Fortunately, my occupational choices have allowed this.

At that time, I was in construction. I never considered myself a construction worker who wanted to be in entertainment. I always thought I was an entertainer stuck in construction. The guys I worked with were nice enough and I got along with them, but they were nothing like me. I knew I was different. I wasn't supposed to be doing this.

Sure, it paid the bills, but I was miserable and did the least amount of work I could possibly do while still keeping my job. Oh, I was very creative at not working. I could bullshit with the best of them. This was back when everyone used beepers. My beeper went off and I'd have to call the boss and be like, "What? Uh, this is just a clusterfuck that you sent me to." Meanwhile, the job was already finished. There were times I got beeped when I was already driving home. The job would take three hours and I would write it as if it were an eight-hour job. The rest of the day I'd be drinking at the bar or riding my jet ski on company time. But I was in a rut and knew I had to do something, anything, to get out of it.

During this time, I was constantly in bands with Joe. I was the front man, the lead vocalist. I always wanted to make it as a musician, but I wasn't delusional. I knew how difficult it was to make any real money at it. I've seen it happen with other people, but within a year they were back working the same old jobs again. It's just the hardest thing to sustain.

I never realistically thought to myself, "Hey, I'm gonna be a rock star!" I was just hoping in some way that this could lead me into something where I didn't have to wake up at 7:30 in the morning and swing a fucking hammer. I needed out of that.

I would write song parodies all the time for my family and friends. My brother would bring his acoustic guitar, and my other friend would have a small drum kit. We'd go out to where my parents would hang out with all their friends at Watch Hill, down on Fire Island. They'd all take their big boats out there, and we'd set out on the dock and play these song parodies, and they fucking loved them!

The people on the dock—people we didn't even know—were laughing their balls off. We'd cover anything that was in the news, like Amy Fisher and Joey Buttafuoco. We did a parody with the Pure Prairie League song "Amie":

"Amie, what ya gonna do? Go out and buy a twenty-two. Put some lead in Mary Joe and now you're through."

And we did one about John Wayne Bobbitt to an old Bee Gees tune:

"You don't know what it's like, baby you don't know what it's like, to lose your penis, to lose your penis, the way I lost mine."

At that point, my brother and I had been doing pretty well with the band thing. We weren't making a lot of money but were making a buzz around town. We both still did our day jobs to pay the bills but were also gigging regularly around New York. My brother was the real go-getter in this whole operation. I was a lazy fuck. Joe was the guy who was motivated to do shit.

In 1994, when the O. J. thing was all over the news, I wrote a parody about it with the song "(Sittin' on) the Dock of the Bay," and it was gonna electroshock O. J.

"Sitting in Los Angeles jail, and that judge won't let me post my bail. Now this could be the end of me, 'cuz California got the death penalty. They gonna electroshock O. J., cook my behind like a cherry flambé. They gonna electroshock O. J, toast my behi...hi...ind."

Silly me, I thought he might get the death penalty for killing two people, and I wrote this song before the verdict came out, but the response was tremendous, and it was relevant and funny. So Joe sent the O. J. parody out to several radio stations in Connecticut, New Jersey, Long Island, and NYC. Stations started playing it, and people loved it! Opie played it and got in touch with us and said, "Guys, I love what you're doing here with this stuff. Come on my show and play it live. Would you do that?" I was like, "Fuck yeah!" Greg "Opie" Hughes was *the* guy in Long Island radio. He was on the major rock station WBAB and did *The Nighttime Attitude*, a show from 7:00 p.m. to midnight. He was a big deal in that market. Everyone on Long Island knew him. He was a real disc jockey who was playing tunes that every Long Island douchebag in a Chevelle wanted to hear as they were drinking and speeding down the expressway.

This was the summer of 1994. I was thinking, "This is it! This is all I needed. I just need this one fucking break. I'm finally going to be on a real radio station because of something I did and wrote. I'm now getting my chance to shine."

Finally, my brother and I were going to the studio to perform live. I would sing and Joe would accompany me on guitar. I had always said I just wanted a chance. "Just let me in there, and if I suck, throw me the fuck out." I didn't want to go to the Columbia School of Broadcasting and learn how to wire a transmitter. You can't teach what works on the radio.

So, we went to WBAB and performed live. We hit it out of the park! Opie thought it was great. I loved it, but by the time the song was finished, I realized there was plenty of time left and I wasn't gonna shut my fucking mouth. I decided to be one of those juggling, spinning-plates guys who plays drums with their feet. I couldn't spit enough shit out onto the show that night. I did impressions, I talked about current events, and Opie was just like, "Who the fuck is this guy?" He was going back and forth with me, and we were having a great time. The show ended, and he said, "Holy shit! Can you come back next week?" Of course, I could come back next week. I'd be there whenever he wanted me.

We continued doing that, and I would read the paper that day at work. I'd go to Opie's show and just start riffing about the news and do impressions and whatever else I could do. I was just happy to be there. I just loved sitting behind that microphone and was just like, "My God, I'm really doing radio now." This was exactly what I wanted to do.

He started inviting me in two days a week, then three days a week, and he was recording all of these shows. All jocks record their shit for air checks, but he was sending the recordings out to stations all over the country. The morning show at WBAB—hosted by Bob Buchmann, who was also a huge name in rock radio on Long Island—started getting wind that Opie had this guy who was doing impressions. He started going into Opie's tape bin and pulling out stuff we had done the night before and started playing it on his show. Opie was getting pissed, but Bob was also the station's program director. So, he couldn't really lay into him. Opie told me about this, but I had already known. I remember I was in an attic cutting a nine-by-nine vent in the ceiling listening to Buchmann on WBAB in the morning. *Bam!* There was me on the radio doing some impression of something newsworthy at the time.

I was sweating, I had the shingle nails hitting me in the head, I was breathing in insulation, and I was hearing my voice on the radio and thinking, "Why am I on the radio and still here?" I couldn't fathom it.

I was on the radio; shouldn't I be rich? So, Opie told me, "I think Bob is going to approach you to do his show." And soon enough, Bob did approach me to do his show, and I did a couple before Opie said, "I'm not going to tell you what to do or anything." The shows didn't go very well. I had no chemistry with the guy. Bob didn't know how to segue into what I did. He'd be like, "Hey, Anthony, look at this news story about Newt Gingrich and…go!" I was like, "What am I supposed to do with that?"

When Opie said, "He's going approach you for the show full time," I said no. I knew I had a better shot with Opie, but I also knew I had to go to work. Opie's show was at night, and Bob's was in the morning, when I had my real job that was paying the bills.

During this time while I was doing Opie's show, we started becoming friends. The first time he invited me over to his house was huge to me. What Howard Stern was to NYC, Opie was to the smaller market of Long Island. If you listened to Howard in the morning and lived on Long Island, you listened to Opie from 7:00 p.m. to midnight. It was just him playing rock and roll and in between songs getting in some funny shit. During that time, he had what was considered a wild show. He'd have girls come in or someone with a goat. It sounds innocent, but we're talking the early nineties, when crazy radio was Stern.

Opie was definitely doing his own thing and had built a nice fan base. So going to his house was no little thing for me. I was so naive about everything. I had my own little world, and that was all I knew. I considered myself very smart, but I was a high school dropout.

I wasn't a stupid person, not by far. I knew a lot about astronomy, physics, and chemistry, but I didn't have the academic credentials to say, "Hey, I'd like a position with you here at IBM! Whatcha got?" I was self-taught about many things but, man, was I naive about life.

Opie invited me over to his house, and I was conjuring all these horrible thoughts of traveling over there in my '86 Dodge Aries K, breaking down, rims of different colors, with smoke pouring out of the car. Thinking I was going to be pulling up to a gate with an intercom saying, "I'm here to see Opie," with the gate opening up to a mansion. I mean, hell, he was on the radio. My assumption was that anyone in any aspect of show business was rich. That's what I honestly thought.

For all the people I knew who listened to Opie, and the fact that he was popular, he had to be a millionaire. So, he gave me his address, and it was in Northport, Long Island, which is a pretty nice fucking area. I pulled up at the address and was like, "Hey, these houses kinda look like shit." I didn't get it. They were just old sea-town Northport houses, broken down because the salt air had fucked with everything. I pulled up to his house and Opie was there waving to me. I was completely disillusioned and confused. In my head—again, Mr. Naiveté—I was like, "This must be his summer home." I mean, the guy had his own radio show from 7:00 p.m. to midnight. Now, in hindsight, I know those guys can't pay their fucking rent doing seven to midnight at a local station.

I went in there and we watched the movie *The Crow* and talked about radio. He talked about how psyched he was about this whole thing. It wasn't even *Opie and Anthony* at this point, but he just loved what I was doing—loved what I was bringing to the show and wanted to expand on it. He really thought we had a chance to go further than WBAB. I was just listening to this and my jaw was on the floor. I couldn't imagine this was an actual thing.

We ended up going to a bar in Northport, and later we always thought of this as "the Big Summit." We kind of carved out what we wanted to do as a radio team, which inevitably became the *Opie and Anthony* show. I took it with a grain of salt, because I had no confidence in what I did. Why would I? I had never done it. I knew what I was to people like my friends, family, and anyone who would listen. But I never knew I had the ability to actually take it pro. I remember him saying, "Hey, Anthony, I love what we're doing here. I want to take the recordings of what we're doing and start sending them out to various radio stations and get us a radio gig. Would you actually be able to leave what you're doing? Because the radio business is weird. You may have to move somewhere and do this." Of course, I said yes! Little did I know that he already had been sending out our recordings.

CHAPTER 7

The Boston Party

Seven months after I first went on Opie's show, he got a tug on the hook from a station in Boston, WAAF. So, we got the opportunity to go to Boston and interview with the general manager, a fella named Bruce Mittman. We drove up there and Opie wasn't telling me things to do, but he filled me in on what program directors and general managers were, because I was clueless. I didn't own a nice suit, so I was wearing a blazer, looking like Crazy Eddie's pitchman. Just really terrible, and I'm sure it was something that might have been somewhat presentable ten years prior.

We got up there and met with Bruce in his nice big corner office. We sat down and I just started doing my act. I was juggling and spinning plates again! I just wanted to show this guy this was what I did. I couldn't sit there and spill out a résumé full of experience. What was I going tell him? "Yeah, I'm a tin knocker and I'm in a band." I knew I had to show this guy what I'd do on the air, not show him a résumé or a list of references. I had to do what I would do on the radio for this motherfucker in front of his face.

I started fitting in impressions and jokes and riffing on things that were happening in the news that day. I did everything. Opie carried the "I'm the radio guy with a résumé. I graduated from college and have a show on WBAB." I was the guy who showed him what I'd do on the air. I was doing really well. I had this internal dialogue going as words flew out of my mouth. I was constantly assessing what I was doing as I was doing it: "Oh, this is good! I hope he likes this." We got done with the interview; he loved us, and he shook our hands. He said, "We'll give you a call and let you know what's going on."

Opie and I got back in his vehicle, and he was ecstatic. I didn't know success from a hole in the wall, but Opie was like, "Dude, you fucking nailed that! That was unbelievable!" I had no clue. We drove all the way back, and he was excited. I was excited for how excited he was. He dropped me off where I was living, which was the second floor of a house that my wife and I were renting. A total piece of shit. Opie got home and called me up and said, "Bruce left me a message on my machine already. If we want the job, we have it." It was that quick. By the time we drove back from Boston to New York, it had already been decided and we had the offer for the job. I couldn't believe it. Opie said, "Bruce will be calling you soon to go over some details," and I was like, "Uh, okay."

Now I started getting really nervous, because I'd never left New York to do anything aside from living in California with my dad when I was kid. This was my first time venturing out without my family and friends to do something out on my own. I had my wife, but that doesn't count. I was petrified. I was thirty-four years old, and my dream was coming true overnight like a freight train. I was in a complete state of, "This can't possibly be happening." I thought I was going to be a fifty-year-old construction worker. Was this a dream? I was making twenty-eight thousand five hundred dollars a year knocking tin at the time.

Bruce Mittman called me and said, "You and Opie are amazing. We knew the second you left the studio that you'd gotten the job." I don't think we were even out of the parking lot when they decided we'd gotten the gig. They immediately decided we were their new afternoon show. He said, "We're gonna give you twenty-seven thousand five hundred dollars to start. But let me tell you something, after six months if you guys have two good books, we'll raise that up and you'll be very happy." The "books" are ratings books, and the ratings are given every three months. Jocks live and die by the ratings books. I didn't care. It was a thousand dollars less than I was making. Who cared? We had an opportunity that was limitless, unlike working for an air-conditioning company, where I was hoping for…what? A quarter raise or something else you get when you're in construction?

I hung up and told Jennifer, "We're going to Massachusetts. I got the gig, and I'm making twenty-seven thousand five hundred dollars." She was like, "What? Call him back and tell him you need to make at least what you're making now." I was like, "Honey, do you understand the opportunity I have? This is one of those life crossroads that you'll remember forever. This isn't 'Should I be working at the Broadway Deli in Greenlawn or the record store-slash-thrift shop?' It's a career, and you're going to quibble over a thousand fucking dollars a year?" She was fucking brutal, and I did everything I could not to argue with her.

I did a make-believe call and pretended to negotiate, and I told Jennifer he agreed to give me a thousand bucks more to equal my current yearly salary. I knew she wasn't going look at my checks and understand taxes and everything else. Anyway, who gave a shit at that point? I was like, "Shut the fuck up; I'm gonna be doing radio."

I didn't care about my debt, my shit car, or my wife. I was refocused and reenergized. I was finally getting paid to be on the radio and knew that was what I was intended to do. It was divine intervention. I was always good at making people laugh and doing a shitload of impressions, and I had a distinct point of view. Now I was going to be making a living at it. I was out of my rut!

We got the job in March, and Bruce Mittman said, "Hey, guys, we're going to give you money for the move." Now, I didn't have much to move. So, instead of calling a moving company, I rented a Ryder van and had my friends help me. My one buddy was like, "Why the fuck didn't you hire a moving company? They would do all this for you."

"They do that?" I didn't even know. I had no idea that was even an option.

That was some foreshadowing of how little I knew about any other aspect of life other than being a construction worker on Long Island. I never knew other things were available. I kept that Dodge Aries K until it broke down. I could have bought a new car; it just never occurred to me. All these new things, having some kind of money and security, never occurred to me. I was horrible with money and the handling of it. If I hadn't gotten a great radio gig that paid unbelievable amounts of money, I'd still be paying off a jet ski I bought in 1992. I couldn't have paid it off otherwise. Companies had sent me credit cards, and I got a jet ski because that's what you do. Isn't it?

We were successful in Boston really quickly. When we had gotten the gig, the program director and manager sat us down and said, "Look, Boston is kinda like this. The last thing you should do is try to make like you're a Red Sox fan, because they will smell phoniness a thousand miles away. We're not saying you should say you're a Yankees fan either. Don't try and fool the audience." Very quickly we decided to play that I was a Yankees fan and Opie was a Red Sox fan, and it worked. Opie was actually a Mets fan, but who gives a shit? They loved the dynamic of having a Red Sox fan and a Yankees fan able to yell at each other on a show, like they love doing in the bar.

It worked out well and we knew it. We knew it more than the general manager (GM) or program director ever would. That was the first instance of many of our knowing better than the management how our show should be. They said, "Don't be confrontational" and, "Don't make fun of the music." We didn't make fun of it, but we wanted to be able to comment on it. They'd get so upset about the littlest things. We started cutting records out of the show so we could talk more. The GM would come in and say, "Uh, boys, are we a talk show now?" Opie would retort, "Are you asking us to be?" He would reply, "Not yet."

They saw where we were going. We weren't meant to sit there and spin records. We were meant to do a talk show, having interesting guests and callers and doing bits. They didn't get that as quickly as we did. I was untainted by what the business was supposed to be. I just thought, "Wow, it would be great if we could do this." I didn't know it was against the rules to throw records away. I'd suggest, "Let's cut these two out, and we can talk more on air."

The fan base in Boston was really picking up on it and loved it. We would do appearances with the entire radio station—the morning, midday, and evening jocks—and there would be a line of people who wanted autographs and pictures with us, much more so than with the other jocks. We had a huge buzz and were really becoming a sensation in Boston. The station was aware of it, but it was in the managers' best interest not to crow about it too much with contracts coming up.

After six months, we were doing exceptionally well, and Bruce Mittman had not lied. He boosted my pay to thirty-six thousand dollars. Opie was making more money than I was at the time, and deservedly so. He was the real "radio guy," and I was thrilled to be essentially learning on the job and being paid. I was and always will be grateful to him for the opportunity and situation he put me in. That said, he knew I was an asset to him as well. I brought certain qualities to the show that made what we accomplished special. He knew that just as much as he had changed my career, I had changed his too. He knew he would not be on this road if I weren't with him, and the same applied to him for me. This combination had to work on so many levels. I had to be funny and get along with him, and we had to be able to tolerate each other's bullshit. When we moved on in our careers after Boston, we always made exactly the same salary. Cent for cent.

We complemented each other perfectly. He would end a song with, "That was the Foo Fighters, and Ant, what's going on today?" I'd have my newspaper in front of me and be off to the races bantering. We'd just start talking, and if we had a guest, we'd introduce the guest. Girls would call up, and we'd tell them to come down to the studio. We did something called the "Blue Tarp Cabaret"—we'd put out a blue tarp, and the girls would get completely naked and we'd throw maple syrup on them. These disgustingly sticky girls, who were hot as shit, would just be smashing each other with cakes and assorted pastries. We'd get the food products from local bakeries and advertise these bakeries like a real plug: "These cakes were supplied by Mom and Pop's Pastries." It was great.

The radio station didn't know what the fuck to do. We tried a lot of new things. There was a lot of stuff people weren't doing on radio at that time. We just had this rapport with each other and with the audience. We never made ourselves sound like those jocks who were bigger than life and better than the audience. We were just two assholes from Long Island trying to make funny radio and get chicks.

We never said we were married or had girlfriends, which pissed my wife off terribly. I didn't want to be a married guy on a young rock station. So, whenever we went out to do these station appearances, there were constantly girls around us. I remember we did one appearance with Kahlúa girls, who wanted us to go skinny-dipping with them in a lake. Opie was like, "I can't," and I was just like, "Fuck!"

I still regret not doing that.

After the first year, we knew it wasn't a fluke. People were loving it, and we started acting accordingly. We knew we could get away with a lot of shit that jocks without ratings couldn't get away with. So, we started doing the show we wanted to do. Before that, we had a program director (PD) named Dave Douglas. Just an awful PD. I don't think it was his fault particularly. He came from the Midwest and thought he was going to bring this hometown old-school mentality to the station.

Dave worked directly under Bruce Mittman. He didn't understand what we were doing or why it was working. He just wanted us to spin records and do one-liners between songs. Nothing more, nothing less. We had to air-check with him every week. We'd have to take a show we'd done and sit there and play it on a cassette. He'd stop and say, "Well, here I think you should have done this and you shouldn't mention this before you go into the read of the advertisement."

Our show was so unique and odd that an air check didn't work with a program director. What was he going to tell us to improve on? It made no sense to have someone structurally critique the show. Structurally, it was a disaster. It was supposed to be. We had to go to the meetings regardless and sit with him and smile. Then we'd go back and do exactly what we knew worked.

This Dave Douglas guy was always just a bug up our asses. He once said, "You know what you should do? Take a picture of who you envision as an audience member. Who do you picture? Find a magazine with a picture of someone who resembles this person you have in mind and put that picture in front of you on your mixing board. So when you're talking into the mic, you get an image of who you're talking to." The fucking guy actually said this! Well, we nodded and smiled, and I couldn't look at Opie and he couldn't look at me at this point. We were just laughing our fucking asses off.

We went on the air, and we just started talking about the meeting and how what he'd said was so ludicrous and idiotic. It was. Then we found a *Swank* magazine and cut out pictures of a woman squatting and posted the pictures. "Here's how we picture our audience: a bunch of filthy cunts." Obviously, we didn't say "cunt." We'd substitute the initial for the word and say "a bunch of Cs." Dave was so pissed that his sound, fatherly advice was just laughed at and patronized.

Henceforth, that became the dynamic for Dave Douglas and the *Opie and Anthony* show. He would tell us stuff sincerely like a boss, a father figure, and we would mock it. This happened week in and week out. He told us not to discuss "gay things." He poked his head in the door while we were recording something. Opie didn't stop recording. We weren't live on the air at that time, and Dave went, "You really want to go into the gay zone as much as you are?" We were like, "What do you mean?" He was like, "Well, you're kind of going into the gay zone. Maybe we should stay clear of that and find another road to go up?" That night we stayed in the studio with the tape of him talking to us. We cut it up and made it into a techno song while putting the gayest music behind it. It was like, "We're going into the gay zone. The ga-ga-ga-ga-gay zone." Dave was so pissed off, but the listeners loved it.

We were the crazy jocks who didn't listen to their boss, and he was the bad guy. It wasn't a cliché version of it or an act. We were fucking with this guy really bad, and our listeners absolutely relished it. Dave would bring us into his office, and it was as if we'd reverted to middle school and were going to see the principal. We would give him inane, child-like excuses. He'd tell us, "I'm the boss. You need to listen to me!" We knew the more nuts the show was, the better it would be—unlike a program director-driven show.

There wasn't another show like it. On any other afternoon-drive radio show was a DJ playing music trying to sound like a hack boss-jock with that corny staged over-the-top broadcaster voice. Then you had these two fucking maniacs who had no business being on the radio talking like real people. We just took off. We were becoming celebrities and pissing off people who didn't like this type of entertainment. We were consistently number one in our demo. We even got some of the older male listeners who would never have been listening to our music but gravitated to our humor.

Boston is a funny fucking city, and Bostonians like raw humor. They love a good filthy off-color joke, and we gave them that type of humor on the radio. We knew how to stretch shit out where we could and just barely squeak past FCC rules. We would use the first letter of curse words. I'd "F" her in the "A" and wipe my "D" on her curtains. It was shocking to people to hear that come out of their radios at that time.

☙

When we were getting set to move to Boston, my wife's mother was already living in Ashland, Massachusetts. I could only concentrate on doing the radio show, and Jennifer handled everything else. This included her idea of living with her mother until we got more settled and found a place of our own. Opie thought the same thing. Opie, Jennifer, and I were living with my mother-in-law, Judy, in a small town house.

Judy was constantly hammered off her ass, saying, "How are yas today, boys?" She slurred her words while stirring her drink simultaneously. My wife and her mom would fight like mothers and daughters do. Jennifer was in her late twenties at the time and still didn't have her driver's license. Her mom was super pissed that Jennifer didn't have a license, but then you would have had two drunks on the road. They'd constantly argue over what to watch next on the TV. Just drunken bantering, like, "Mom, you know we need to watch *General Hospital* before *Oprah*!" "Are you out of your fucking mind, Jennifer? We need to rewind the tape first and watch Friday's episode we missed." "Fine, where's the mixer? We need to go for a liquor run before I get too fucked up to drive."

Jennifer wanted to get out of there as quickly as possible but stay close to her mom. We moved into a garden apartment in Ashland that was just horrible, and Opie continued living with my mother-in-law for another six months. Just the weirdest setup. But my wife and I continued to live in Ashland the entire time we lived in Massachusetts. Once again, I didn't care. All I cared about was doing that show. I didn't care if I lived in a box or who I was with. Three to 7:00 p.m. was all that I lived for the whole time I was out there, and I loved it.

We used to have to do "production." It's like when you first get a job in radio, you have to do the commercials. They'll give you a script, and it'll be like, "This is for Newbury Comics. Come down to Newbury Comics and get blah blah blah at this price" and you'd add the address with a musical tag. I'd have to put it together on the tape machine, literally tape back then. I loved it. The show would end at 7:00 p.m. and I'd be in there until 10:00 or 11:00 p.m. sometimes. I'd do a voice or some bullshit. I wanted to get it just right. The production guy was like, "I love what you're doing. This is great."

I started noticing that my stack of production items I had to do after the show was filling up my little cubicle and Opie's pile was going down. They called Opie "Slappy." He'd just run through his copy with apathy and zero enthusiasm. Bam. Done. Gone. Fifteen minutes and he was finished. Meanwhile, I was tracking shit and making it sound great. The production guy actually submitted one of my spots for some radio advertisement award, and it won. I received a glass statuette thing with a glass plate with my name on it. I was really proud of it. I think my wife threw it in the fireplace after I divorced her. My first real radio award. Hey, these things happen.

Opie, who was already a seasoned radio pro, said he "never saw any radio team work as successfully and as quickly" as we did. Boston was where we culminated and eventually came into what we wanted to be. We both went through so much there that by the time we came back to NYC to sign a new contract with WNEW-FM, for the first time I felt like an equal to Opie.

We signed a package deal with us both getting 145,000 dollars, which was really good money for me back then. So, we shared equal billing and even had a clause in our contract that if one of us were to be fired, the other one would be too. We even had to take vacations at the same exact time. We did the show as a team or we didn't do it at all. Early on we even took a few vacations together.

Our friendship in the early years was very strong. Initially it was a little weird for me, because it's very hard to immediately have a friendship with someone you're intimidated by. He was doing well in a business I wanted to do well in. I was very envious of his job. Not jealous or vindictive, but he was doing what I would have loved to be doing. It's very hard to build a friendship off that. I looked at him and myself as being on such different levels. Once we started working together and I started getting recognized by the fans at WBAB as someone who was really doing well and helping the show, and I started to get to know Opie as person and not just a "radio guy," that gap started closing. I'd say three to four months after coming on his show, I felt like we were becoming real friends.

At the very beginning it was self-serving, because I didn't want to fuck things up. I had my foot in the door and needed to keep it open. So if he said, "Hey, can you be there this day or that day?" I made it happen. I was already pissing off my brother, as well as the other guys in the band. We'd have rehearsals and I'd be like, "I'm doing the *Opie* show." And I'd hear, "Oh, you're not dedicated to the band now."

There was a lot of animosity between me and the guys. They wanted total dedication to the band and I was finding a way out, which retrospectively was the best choice I've ever made. They were really upset when I told them I was moving to Boston to do a radio show. My brother, Joe, said to me at one point, "So you're gonna fucking play around on the radio when you have something really great here with the band?" I still goof on him about that! There's nothing better than when you can turn the screw on your older brother like that. "Oh really, Joe?" Joe obviously knew very quickly that I had made the right decision.

I knew I was starting to do well when I cleared my twenty-two thousand dollars' worth of credit card debt. I'd be getting credit cards in the mail like they were dealing out poker chips. You'd get a ten thousand-dollar limit and say you'd use it for emergencies only. Then a jet ski later and you're looking into selling your kidney to pay off the interest. I was in Boston, and I wrote a check to three different credit card companies and paid off every credit card bill. That was one of the few fond memories I have of my wife. We opened a bottle of champagne and I said, "I can't believe I just paid off something that I never, not even in my wildest hallucinations, ever thought I could possibly do."

That told me we are really going places.

CHAPTER 8

The Mayor Is Dead

IN 1998, OPIE AND I were at the height of our popularity in Boston. We were into our third year at WAAF FM and number one in the ratings book, consistently beating our competition by a landslide for our target audience. The station intended for us to play music, and up until this point we had never officially done a real talk show.

The breaks got longer, and we started dropping a lot more songs. The hour, which originally started with twelve songs, went down to six and we'd talk the rest of the time. The more we talked, the higher our ratings went. The PD didn't know what to do. He came into the studio one day and said, "Are we a talk-radio show now?" I replied, "Yeah, I think we are." Within a year it metamorphosed into a full-time talk show known as the *Opie and Anthony* show. It was clear that our audience wasn't tuning in for the music. They were listening to hear what Opie and I were going to say or do next.

April Fools' Day was a perfect example of how we could separate ourselves from our competition. We'd usually goof on every other jock's attempt at a bad April Fools' prank. We marveled at how anyone could ever fall for these transparent hoaxes. It was always something so ridiculously stupid, like, "There's going to be a meteor at noon today. So, when the clock strikes twelve and you look up, you'll see a meteor." Come on, man, does anyone believe that shit? Another jock would say, "We're changing our format to all Elvis songs." They'd play two Elvis songs and say, "April Fools!" It was so lame. If you want to do that, do it till midnight. People would be like, "I know it's April Fools' but, fuck, are they really doing this?"

On one particular April 1, Opie decided he wanted to do something really outrageous and ridiculous that no one would ever believe. Early that morning he called me up, giddy as a schoolgirl, and said, "I got it!" I was literally half asleep, in that state where you're awake but also so groggy, you're practically dreaming your own consciousness. "You got what?" I muttered. "An April Fools' gag!" he said. "We're going to say mayor Tom Menino is dead." I was like, "Great. Sounds cool. I'll see ya later." And went right back to sleep.

Later that day, I got into the studio and Opie and I started game-planning the situation. Even though I hadn't been doing radio very long, my radar went off that this could be real trouble. The thing is, we were always in trouble, and whatever we did that was deemed controversial translated into more popularity among our fans. It never occurred to me to say, "We shouldn't do this," because trouble was great! If you're in the shock jock radio game, trouble is absolutely what you're looking for.

The mayor was in Florida at the time, and Opie came up with a scenario that he'd been involved in a car accident that resulted in his death. April Fools! Opie knew a guy at WBAB with an amazing broadcaster voice and got him to call into our show as the "news guy," giving us the story with all the facts behind the tragedy of the mayor's fabricated fatal vehicular homicide. It was set up very convincingly, but the goal was to have it snowball into something ludicrous and ridiculous. As the details came in, we intended to make them so unbelievable that everyone would know it was obviously an April Fools' prank.

Opie got on the air and said, "We're getting some news about Mayor Menino in Florida. Just stay tuned; we'll come back after a few more songs." Opie looked at me and I looked at him. We had just officially pushed the "go" button for this prank.

The next break we came on and said, "We unfortunately have some tragic news that Mayor Menino has been killed in a car crash in Florida. We're getting details right now and will get you those as soon as we come back from this next break. Once again, it is confirmed: Mayor Menino is dead."

We were feeling weird about it because we knew some people would be losing their minds over this news. We knew where it was going and that our listeners would soon realize it was a prank.

As soon as we made the initial announcement that the mayor of Boston was dead, our program director, Dave Douglass, came into our studio. We referred to him as "Dave Dickless." Dave never had our back on anything we did that could be perceived as controversial or outside the box of normality—the very things that were making us the toast of the town and increasing the numbers in our listening audience. After three years, Dave Dickless was figuratively castrated by us and our shenanigans. He would tell us, "Don't you dare do this. We're getting flooded with letters and complaint calls." The second he would leave, we would purposely do exactly what he had just told us not to do.

He'd come back in screaming during the commercial break, and we'd just pretend there had been a miscommunication, saying, "Oh, we thought you meant that *specifically*." He'd scream, "You know goddamn well what the fuck I meant!" His face would be bright red, and we thought his head was going to fucking explode.

Dave came running into the studio right after we announced that the mayor had died in a car crash, and said, "Okay, guys, what are you doing?" We explained it was just an April Fools' bit. He said, "I'm not sure about this one. I don't like the way this could go." We tried to put him at ease, "Relax, Dave, the audience is going to realize soon enough that this is a prank with our outrageous details." He was like, "Okay, just watch yourselves with this one."

He left, and we came back on air with our broadcasting ringer from WBAB with the Ted Koppel voice, who sounded very newsworthy, to confirm the car crash, and he just nailed it.

We then said someone else had been killed with the mayor in his car. "Just getting this news: the passenger in the mayor's car, who was also killed, was a young Haitian boy." We wanted to lead up to the fact that he had been having sex in the car with this young Haitian boy while driving and the car had spun out of control.

We never got to this point. The second we got done with our last report with our fake news correspondent, Dave Dickless burst into the studio and said, "We have to knock this off. We're starting to get calls from the news stations and concerned citizens asking if this is true. Ya gotta stop this now!"

We didn't want to just say, "April Fools." That's hacky bullshit and is exactly what we didn't want to do. So we refused to say it but assured Dickless we'd stop speaking about it. We left it hanging there, in what was probably the most believable phase of it. If we would have been allowed to continue and make it seem stupid, people would have realized it was fake news and a prank. Dickless made us stop right after we said the mayor was dead.

Before the end of the show, we saw the news ticker on the bottom of the Fox 25 news say, "DJs claim Mayor Menino is killed." Opie saw this and went, "Uh-oh." We knew it wouldn't stop there, and this was really going to be something that would snowball into this huge thing before it finally went away. I was naive; at the time I was thinking, "Great, we did it. We made the news!" Not a good thing.

After the show we were brought in for a meeting with our general manager, Bruce Mittman, and Dickless. They told us how they wanted this handled. They informed "Rocko the DJ," the jock on our station who had a show after us, to announce it was an April Fools' joke, which he did. No one listened to Rocko, so who cared? No one heard it, and it was already out of the bag. The news had already started running with what we'd said, and it was now becoming a big local story.

The next day we came into work and went on the air discussing it. Every news station wanted to interview us, and we were informed to not speak with any press. Bruce and Dave said they would prefer to handle it. We got done with the show that day and went out to the elevators, waiting for the doors to open. From out of the lunchroom came a camera guy and a local news anchor, shouting, "What do you have to say to Mayor Menino and his family? They thought he was dead because of your prank yesterday. Do you have any regret? Are you sorry?" Opie replied first, saying, "I didn't realize the mayor's family was fans of the O and A show." I just rolled my eyes in a sarcastic and patronizing way and said, "Alright, we apologize to the mayor's family." I was so insincere, and we made an already tumultuous situation worse. Dickless and Bruce were right about one thing: they should have handled this for us.

We were actually psyched about being on the news that night. This was great publicity for a shock jock show. The piece aired and now the mayor's office was livid. Mayor Menino said his family heard it and really thought he was dead. I went on record saying I didn't believe it, because "you don't go to CNN for dick jokes, and you don't listen to O and A for real news." Things just escalated, and the mayor demanded we get fired.

We were the scourge of society and especially internally at the station with "Whip 'Em Out Wednesday," the sex, and the other shit we pulled on the air that rubbed people the wrong way. When we killed the mayor, it really pissed off a lot of people. Mittman and Dickless came up with an idea to make us more likable.

They wanted to publicly have us make amends for our sins. They said, "We'd like you guys to get in a stockade, and we'll buy a bunch of pies and have the mayor throw pies at your face. Opie and I were like, "There's no fucking way we're ever gonna do that. Are you out of your mind? Do you think this is Nebraska local radio? No, we are not doing it." They insisted, "Yes, you are doing this!" Opie said, "What does the mayor have to say about this?" He had to sign off on it, and we knew he would never do it. We'd said he was dead; his family was traumatized. Would you think he would agree to let bygones be bygones with a pie in the face?

They of course tried to facilitate this with the mayor, and he pretty much told them to go fuck themselves and wondered when these assholes were going to be fired. Here's the best part: while they were waiting for the mayor to answer them, they bought the pies. Not a couple but a whole fuck load of pies! So, once the mayor vehemently turned down their offer, they had to do something with all these pies. They came up with another brilliant idea to make us look likable. They wanted us to go to Boston Children's Hospital and give the pies to little cancer kids. Opie and I once again were thinking, "You soulless motherfuckers. You want us to go down and use terminally ill children to get our shock jock jobs back?" We said, "No, we are not doing that."

"Well, we already set up that you guys were going to deliver the pies to the kids," Bruce and Dickless told us. We said, "Look, we'll be more than glad to go to the hospital and deliver the pies and spend time with the kids. That said, if we see any press, we're gonna punch them right in the fucking face. This is not to be for public consumption."

We delivered the pies and spent time with the kids, but there was no press about it. These two geniuses were out of ideas to save our jobs and increase our likability. Bruce actually made one last attempt, which was to stalk the mayor and jump out, then shake the mayor's hand while having a photographer get a picture. They did get the picture, and it was in the paper. It was captioned something like, "GM of shock jock shaking hands with Mayor Menino saying fire them." It was a clusterfuck with them trying to salvage our jobs. Everyone made bonuses with our high ratings, and sales were up. They could charge more money for a spot on our show. They didn't want to lose our show, which was making them the most money.

This was a weird time for WAAF, because it was owned by Zapis Communications. At the time, Zapis was selling WAAF to CBS Radio. CBS owned BCN, which was our main competitor, and we were beating the shit out of them. CBS said to fire us, which would allow BCN to be number one again in the afternoons. CBS was the one that really pulled the trigger on our getting canned. They made us go to the Colonnade Hotel for an interview for an internal investigation. A woman was conducting the investigation and told us this was merely a procedural thing and she wanted to get us back on the air right away, which turned out to be bullshit. These types of inquisitions have only one goal, which is to find out who should be fired. We didn't have a prayer. We were done in Boston, and we knew it.

Dave Douglas was suspended for two weeks, and Bruce Mittman was suspended for a month. A guy representative from CBS Radio came in and was the one who actually terminated our contract. He let us know we were being let go effective immediately, and was affectionately named "the Terminator." You could tell the guy loved his job and really enjoyed firing us.

Opie and I were obviously freaked out by this. Opie kind of knew this was part of the business, and I was the one who was like, "Well, it was great while it lasted. Now what am I gonna fucking do?"

Strangely enough, we'd had an interview a month prior with WNEW FM in NYC. They really liked us and wanted to give us the gig. We unfortunately were under contract and not even supposed to be entertaining such meetings. This new program director who'd just come on board with the station was familiar with *O&A* and loved us. He wanted to change the direction of WNEW and start with personality-driven radio like our show.

Shortly after being terminated from our Boston gig, we hooked up with our agent, Robert Eatman. He got in contact with Opie and said he could really help us get the best deal possible with our next gig. Our last year in Boston, I was making eighty-five thousand dollars.

CHAPTER 9

Back with a Vengeance

Many people speculated that we were smart enough to purposely get fired to go to WNEW. We weren't. Was it a subconscious thing? Maybe. We were even being courted by an Atlanta station, 96 Rock, that wanted us to do the morning show. They took us to a strip club and showed us some amazing homes in Buckhead.

They told us there were so many New Yorkers there, it was almost a second New York. This actually played well into our agent Rob's hand, because two stations were bidding against each other.

Our hearts were leading us to the mecca of broadcasting, Manhattan. Before CBS could sign off on their offer, we needed to get the green light from the king of radio broadcasting and the president and CEO of CBS, Mel Karmazin. Opie and I had to fly from Boston to DC. We then took a car ride into the suburbs of Northern Virginia to a small office park, where we sat in a waiting room till this Southern guy could meet with us. He was going to determine whether we were okay to work for CBS Radio after being fired for our stunt in Boston.

We were sitting there for a while until we finally got invited into his office. He said to us, "So, you boys um, all good?" We were like, "Uh, yeah." He said, "No tails or horns out of there?" "Nope. We're cool." He said, "Alright. I'll sign off."

We were in the office for literally thirty seconds and then back in the car to the airport and in the plane heading back to Boston. Opie and I looked at each other and said, "What the fuck just happened?"

WNEW offered us a deal for 145,000 dollars a year each. I really thought I had made it. I was earning what successful doctors and lawyers make a year, and I was also going back to live in New York, my hometown, where I could be around my friends and family, which was a huge plus.

"The Terminator" who had fired us in Boston was actually the same guy who ended up hiring us for WNEW in NYC. Yep, CBS owned WNEW and fired us in Boston so their other channel could flourish, and hired us for NYC, where we could do well in their New York property. It was a win-win for everybody. I honestly think if they'd had nothing to do with Zapis or WAAF, we wouldn't have been fired no matter how much the mayor yelled about it.

Retrospectively, I think it was purely a political move on CBS's part to get us the fuck out of there. We were bitch-slapping BCN, and they wanted us in New York, where we could hold down afternoons after Howard Stern controlled the mornings on their other station.

After being fired in April, we were rehired in July and started our show on WNEW FM in September. This time I hired a moving van. Truth be told, I didn't even take much back to New York. Now that I had money, my wife and I decided to splurge a little and buy some long overdue new shit. You would think Jennifer would be as excited for me as I was. Nope. My wife was a little broken up about moving away from her mom again. Opie and Sandy Delgado, whom Opie was dating at the time, were actually sad to leave Boston as well. They really loved it there. I was thrilled about coming back home to New York.

Jennifer and I rented a house in Huntington, Long Island. It wasn't even a quarter mile away from the house Opie rented. We lived very close to each other and at that time were very close friends. When we'd go through those times of just insanity—a lot of publicity, big-money deals, the firing and hiring—we really did circle the wagons around ourselves. There was a close pack made up of myself, Jennifer, Opie, and Sandy.

This was truly the most exciting time for me in my career. It was still new to me and I wasn't jaded. I enjoyed every second of it, even the shitty parts when we got bitched out by the higher-ups or had personality conflicts with some of the staff. Nothing bothered me career-wise; it was my personal life with my toxic wife that was in turmoil. I'll get to that a little later.

I was thrilled to be working in NYC! Boston was cool. I would tell my family and friends I was well known there, but when I'd come back to New York to visit, nobody gave a shit. I remember a buddy of mine saying, "I was out on Orion Point [Long Island] and I heard this crackly sound, and it was you from WAAF." The idea of my coming back to this huge station that was the pinnacle in NYC, where everyone from Long Island could and would listen to me, was beyond surreal.

Opie and I were pretty cocky, with inflated egos and senses of self-worth. We were like, "They can't get rid of us. The more controversial we are, the better we do. They fire us and in no time we have an even better job for much more money in NYC. This is fucking awesome." Opie and I decided that whenever a boss would tell us what to do, we'd say, "Go fuck yourself!" This methodology had worked perfectly for us up to this point.

The guy who'd originally interviewed us for the job was our new program director, and he was out-of-his-mind nuts. He had ideas for the station that would change by the minute. He wanted these old traditional music jocks who had been there since the seventies to somehow work with the likes of Opie and myself. These guys were the ones who had written books on rock and roll and were able to get quotes from Keith Moon, because they hung out with him.

They were traditionalists and we were pieces of shit who were fucking up the whole medium. When we first got to WNEW, these guys were the upperclassmen who had ruled the roost, and we were these new guys whom they didn't understand. They disliked us immediately.

Our show very much catered to the male audience. We spoke about current events, sex, music, and we'd have listeners who would call us up or come into the studio and do outrageous shit. We'd have a girl who would call in and say, "Hey, I'd like to come in and stick a zucchini up my ass." Alrighty, come on up. They'd come in and we'd try to describe it the best we could. It was always a freak show/circus atmosphere. New York City was obviously the perfect canvas for the debauchery we needed to amuse our listeners.

The timing was advantageous. During that pre-internet era, you could still do outrageous things on the radio and it would be considered crazy. Today I could pick up my phone and in two seconds see a chick blowing a moose. Back then you could describe a woman getting naked in the studio and it was considered really wild. Not to say we didn't do our fair share of crazy shit. We had a girl come in and stick a cellphone up her pussy to see if we could still get it to ring. It did! We could hear the phone ringing and it was hilarious. It was that day that I switched to Verizon. Jesus, they really do get the best reception.

Another thing that worked out timing-wise was that back in the old days, every station had a general manager and a program director right down the hall from the studio. If there was trouble, he'd be there to run in and put out any fires. When CBS started taking over a bunch of radio stations in various markets, they had sectors. They had a Northeast sector. When we joined, they had one GM who would cover WNEW, a station in Philly, and another in DC, and he wasn't around all the time breathing down our backs. This gave us the opportunity to be out of our fucking minds, since we weren't being supervised.

The show became an enormous success really fast. We were climbing the charts and used it to our advantage by twisting the screws on management. Our PD had the biggest office in our studio, and during one of our negotiations, Opie demanded that it belong to us. The PD had to move into our smaller office. We then decked out that workplace with a refrigerator, a full bar, and a computer system I could play games on. I would hang out with our producer, Rick, and interns, Garrett and Ben, sometimes until midnight, partying and playing video games.

Ron Bennington and Fez Whatley were brought in to go on after our show from 7:00 to 11:00 p.m. I loved those guys! They were funny and great to hang out with. Our audience was passionate and loyal, but their audience had this weird, almost cult-like quality. I used to hang out after my show with those guys, because I didn't want to go home to my wife. We would drink and get hammered. They were the ones who could bring the girls up to the studio. Once again, no supervision. This workplace was like a frat house with constant drinking, smoking, drugs, and sex. I used to get laid on my desk in my office.

It was a constant party that in hindsight had to end. There was just too much shit going on. I couldn't imagine another workplace today allowing the flexibility and climate we had then. You hear about these cool places to work today, like Google. "Yeah, it's great here! My boss skateboards down the hallway, and it's wild." I was simultaneously mixing drinks, smoking cigarettes, and getting laid while spitting on skateboarders from my office window. Beat that, Google!

We'd bring pinball machines and foosball tables into our lobby area and be smoking and drinking all throughout the show. We even had a Snapple machine that we filled with beer. I would pop open a Samuel Adams or a Bud and put it behind my monitor. When it was gone, I'd get an intern to get me another. During breaks I'd play foosball or pinball. It was like I was at a fucking bar drinking. This was my job, and I was getting paid very well to party my ass off. The PD didn't give a shit, and the GM was never there. As long as our ratings were kicking ass, they didn't give a shit what we did. Wonderful times.

We thought we were untouchable. If you had ratings, that was it. You were fine. Nothing you said or did on air could get you in trouble with the higher-ups. This train of thought would eventually lead to our demise.

In the second year, we really had a lot going on. We started doing personal appearances, live remotes from bars, and were even featured in magazines like *Maxim* and *Penthouse*.

Penthouse did a big article and photo shoot with us, which was literally a dream come true. I'd been jerking off to that magazine my whole life! Now I was finally going to be in it, and hopefully not having anyone jerk off to *me*.

The photo shoot included a naked model, with Opie and me dressed up like geeky schoolkids. I remember telling my mom that I was going to be featured in a big magazine. I knew she was thinking, "*Time*? *Newsweek*? *National Lampoon*?" "No, Mom, it's *Penthouse*." Hey, at least it wasn't *Hustler*, with some scratch-and-sniff feature. My mom said, "Are you going to be naked?" "No, Mom, I'm fully clothed with a naked girl." "Thank God, Anthony! I'm so proud of you!"

During this time, WNEW FM turned into FM Talk 102.7 and we started getting some interesting guests, but could never get the A-listers because Howard would get them. If Howard got the guest in the morning, then the powers that be didn't want the two shows to share. With Howard getting these A-listers, we were then relegated to what they thought would be the trash heap of the guests, which turned out to be a lot of New York stand-up comics.

The first few guys we had on the show were Rich Vos, Jim Norton, Patrice O'Neal, Nick Di Paolo, Otto & George, and Colin Quinn. It worked out really well for the comics and for us. It was like the comedians' table at the Comedy Cellar, but with microphones. The comics became regulars on our show and started feeling comfortable enough to be themselves, without having to do their acts.

Aside from comics, we had some unique characters come on the show. Case in point: Steve "the Whistler" Herbst. Now, if you tell a radio audience, "We have a guest who whistles," they're gonna turn off the radio. Opie and I had to know how to make these guests interesting. If you can make a guy like this so entertaining that fifteen years later people come up to you and still talk about it, you did something right. This guy, Steve "the Whistler," had won a whistling tournament and we saw he was booked on the show.

Opie and I never really planned what we were going to do with our guests. Ninety percent of the time it was off-the-cuff riffing. We sometimes would have a segment called "Bad Guest Day" or "Has-Been Corner" and would never let the guests know they were part of that type of show. So, Steve "the Whistler" came in and had a music disc that he was going to whistle along with. Opie put the disc in, and Steve was going to whistle live to the musical track. I was sitting there just cringing at this whole thing. The music began, Steve started whistling, and Opie immediately hit the button to stop the disc. Opie said, "Aww man! If we can't get good equipment, how are we supposed to have guests come in? Dammit! Steve, we are so sorry; let's just start again."

Now this is an example of how Opie and I worked very well together, because I knew exactly what he was doing. I was on this. I was playing good cop to Opie's clandestine bad cop. I knew damn well we were never gonna hear this song, which was good. The audience didn't want to hear it, and neither did we. No one wants to hear a fucking guy whistle a song. Opie started it up again, and right when Steve chimed in to start this beautiful whistling, the music abruptly stopped again. Then I jumped in with, "What the hell is going on here?" We had Steve start this song ten fucking times! He honestly believed there was technical difficulties. The audience obviously knew we were messing with this guy, and Steve couldn't be more oblivious and was getting frustrated. He just wanted to jam out in the worst way and show off his prodigious whistling skills. I really didn't think it would last any longer. I seriously thought he was gonna flip out and punch us or something. He was so into the thought that he was on WNEW radio, and wanted to get his song out in the worst way. Steve would put up with anything, and he did.

It got to the point where I couldn't take it any longer. I was literally crying from laughter. I said, "Let me check the wires," because I needed to go behind the equipment and take a second to compose myself. Opie kept a straight face without breaking character. The audience absolutely loved it. This is a great example of the *Opie and Anthony* show that all our fans know and remember us for. It wasn't like, "How'd you like the show today?" "Well, we had Arnold Schwarzenegger on." Then immediately people would think, "Wow, that must've been a great show." It was more like, "How was the show today?" "We had this guy Steve 'the Whistler' on." No one's gonna think that's a great show, but meanwhile fifteen years later, people still come up to me and say, "That fucking guy Steve 'the Whistler' made me laugh my balls off!"

We had the ability to take stuff that normally another radio show wouldn't touch and make it work well. It was all we had to work with at the time. We were a very disrespected show for how well we were doing. This was directly due to Howard Stern's being part of the same company and management's kowtowing to everything he said. Howard was their big moneymaker, and we had to put up with the leftovers. We got very good at working with utter shit to make it funny and entertaining.

Our audience was passionate, and we were smart enough to utilize the internet in its early stages to be in touch with the listeners. We constantly had chat rooms up and running and would upload pictures we could share while doing our show, which connected us with our fans. We let everyone see what we and our studio looked like.

It was like the live streaming of today in its premature state. We called it the "stinky cam" after Garrett, whose nickname was "Stinky." Garrett still works for me today. He found a program that was something like ten frames per minute. Our audience was able to get glimpses of sometimes naked chicks and us doing our thing. The company didn't care what content was going out, because they didn't even know what the internet was at this point. This really helped us ingratiate ourselves with our listeners in a unique way, and they flocked to it. They felt a part of the show.

The fans were crazy, and Opie and I were constantly just trying to feed them what they wanted. It was like, if you didn't feed them, they'd feed on *you*, and we didn't want any part of that.

We developed an assault on the media. Once again, we barely had any resources from our company, which was CBS Radio. "How about a commercial or billboard for our show?" we'd ask. They'd reply, "It's not in the budget." So, we had to make our own publicity.

We had to think outside the box, which led us to the idea of having our fans hold up *Opie and Anthony* signs behind newscasters doing live segments on the street. That way our show out there every night, and it was free advertising.

We fucked up the news media so bad that they started doing their news spots on top of their vans. They were petrified. It started out with us suggesting to fans that they hold up a sign the second they saw a broadcast go live. "Once you see the light go on the camera, just run up with the sign and yell, '*O and A*! *O and A*!'" We'd reward these brave hearts by telling them to come back to the studio after they did it and hang out with us. We'd give them shirts and hats.

What started out with just flashing a sign behind a reporter was taken to the umpteenth level by fans now running in front of the reporter with a sign that had a big cock drawn on it. We fed the audience and in return, they wanted to feed us. They wanted us to recognize their displays of loyalty by mentioning on air, "Oh wow, did you see that guy hold up the *O and A* sign? That was cool." "Well if that was cool, what are they gonna say about me holding a sign with a huge cock on it?" We loved it! We thought it was hilarious. There was a person who made a sign with the word "cunt" that was displayed clear as day on live TV. Sometimes the fan would call us right before doing it. We'd have the news on knowing it was going live soon, and we would have a guy around the corner directing him when to do it. "Okay, go now!"

One time in front of the Ed Sullivan Theater where Letterman was taping, the reporter Marvin Scott was outside doing a piece and we had one of our guys, "Psycho Mark," run right at him yelling, "*O and A!*" Psycho Mark stepped on an ice patch and couldn't stop himself. He went sliding super fast and took out Marvin Scott during the live news segment. The anchor in the studio came on and was like, "Well, that was unexpected; we'll be right back after this commercial."

We did get in a little trouble because some CBS stations got hit with these antics and we were under the same company umbrella. We had to go on the radio and say, "Could you please not do the signs on CBS, because our bosses are getting a little mad." That culminated in somebody taking one of those obnoxiously loud air horns and blaring it directly into a newscaster's ear. A year later this newscaster and his wife, who was also a newscaster, filed a lawsuit against us.

The lawsuit was hilarious. They claimed he suffered a loss of hearing, and his wife sued for lack of sexual relations as a result of this incident. They were suing for millions of dollars. CBS lawyers took over, and I believe they settled for just enough to cover their lawyer fees and possibly a new TV that came with closed captioning. The press we got from all of this was well worth everything on our end.

Our studio was on 57th Street and Seventh Avenue, and as luck would have it, there was a Hooters restaurant conveniently located next door, which is where we did a signing of our *Penthouse* magazine article. These personal appearances would always turn into debaucherous parties with girls getting naked. We would constantly get into trouble with the owner of whichever place was hosting. These owners were fans of the show, and it went from "We love you guys!" to "You can't do that! I'm going to get shut down!"

One time at Hooters, we had two girls take off everything, with just their panties remaining. Guys put a couch on the stage, and these two chicks started making out with each other in their underwear in front of everyone. Opie and I just looked at each other and said, "What the fuck is this? How did we get people to do this?" There was a crowd screaming like it was ancient Rome. They were just loving it, and once again another thing that led to our demise was that we thought it was never good enough. A girl would flash her tits and it was great. Then another girl would come up and they would both get naked and start making out with each other. "Okay, even better, but no, let's take it even further. Get the couch up here so they can lie down. Alright, throw some water on them."

We would always try to bring it up another notch, never thinking anything bad would come of it. The louder the crowd yelled, the more energized we got to try to figure out the next thing we could do to make them yell louder.

We did a personal appearance in Buffalo called "T&A with *O&A*." It was at a bar that was located right on the beach of Lake Erie.

Our idea was to get local strippers and have them play volleyball on the beach. Perfect, right? Sounds like a fun little day out with our fans.

When we got there, the place was packed. Wall-to-wall people in the bar and on the beach. A lot of drinking was going on, and the strippers started playing volleyball. These girls weren't very good. If they could get a volley back and forth three times, it was amazing. Needless to say, no one was watching them for their expertise at the game as much as hoping a tit would pop out of a bikini.

Meanwhile, this was a public area. The local authorities didn't close it off for our event, so there were families with their children on this beach and the inevitable was pending. They weren't right next to the volleyball court, but they could easily see it. Once again, between the boisterous drinking crowd and the strippers with Opie and me at the helm orchestrating ways to take things to another level, these poor civilians with their families never had a chance.

We floated the idea of the strippers taking their tops off, and they couldn't get them off fast enough. Then some guy by the bar area found a bunch of fruits and vegetables. This guy started handing zucchinis and cucumbers to the strippers.

The girls ended up on the sand totally naked, shoving vegetables in one another's vaginas and asses. Now we weren't on the air, but we did have microphones and were doing a play-by-play for everyone, which included the innocent family bystanders who had become involuntary witnesses.

I was like Howard Cosell. "Opie, I can't see that cucumber fitting. Oh my God, it's going in all the way!"

Parents were grabbing their kids and running off the beach like there was a shark attack. It was quite the scene but a hell of a lot of fun.

We got back to Manhattan and heard from our GM that we were in big trouble and that people from Buffalo wanted to arrest us for inciting a riot that included public nudity.

The only thing is, we weren't in Buffalo anymore. There was nothing the Buffalo authorities could do. Regardless, it was strongly suggested to us that we not go to Buffalo for a while. "Say it ain't so. Anything but that. I wanted to summer there!"

The station had to answer a complaint from the FCC about the appearance. What? This was ridiculous! The appearance in Buffalo didn't even air on public radio! How the fuck could the FCC do anything about something that wasn't on the air? The company and their lawyers said, "We're going to go through everything we have to on this." In my recollection and knowledge of the FCC, it was the only time they ever got a complaint about something that wasn't on the radio. We were fired shortly after for a completely different incident, which made this Buffalo one a moot point.

At this time, Opie and I would carpool in from Huntington, Long Island. We'd grab something to eat, discuss the news of the day, and hang out before our show. One particular day, I was served divorce papers from Jennifer at the radio station studio. I had just been starting to put away money and had forty thousand dollars in the bank. My first instinct was to go to the bank and take twenty thousand out. I just wanted my half.

Opie came with me to the bank, and I filled out a withdrawal form. The teller at the bank came back informing me there was no money in this account. Opie just turned his head and gave me some privacy. The thing that pisses me off is that I was taking out twenty thousand and going to do the right thing by leaving her half. This lady who at one time said she'd be with me "till death do us part" had decided to take more than her part. She had taken the whole nest egg, all forty thousand of it. This was all the money I had at the time. Her lawyer had advised her to take all the money out before serving me the divorce papers. Figures, the only smart thing she ever did in our relationship was hire the best divorce attorney. We walked out of the bank and Opie just erupted, laughing his ass off, and said, "Dude, you got so fucked!" I just joined in laughing. I realized it was officially over with Jennifer and worth whatever it would cost, which turned out to be a lot more than forty fucking grand.

CHAPTER 10

Nothing Lasts Forever

THE TRUTH WAS, EVEN while the *O&A* show was successful, Opie and I had personally been treading water for years prior to the actual breakup in 2014, when I was fired from Sirius.

What really caused waves between Opie and me was my divorce and, subsequently, my full-time girlfriend, who caused the divorce in the first place. He resented her, and it created friction between the two of us. She was basically the Yoko Ono in the whole situation.

When we first teamed up, I was married and he wasn't. My wife and his girlfriend got along very well, and we used to do the double-date bullshit: movies, dinners, events, and the like.

To say my divorce from Jennifer disrupted things between Opie and me would be an understatement. Opie liked the stable situation and didn't want anything to fuck it up. But of course, "Johnny Fontaine comes along with his olive oil voice and Guinea charm." I put a monkey wrench in the works by axing the wife and picking up this pretty wild fucking chick.

Let me explain.

I got married in 1991, after Jennifer and I had been dating for only a very short period of time. I was pushed into marrying her. She had her hooks in me and I couldn't say no. So I walked right up to the justice of the peace and said, "I do," knowing full well I *didn't.*

I didn't want to be married to this girl from the get-go, but how could I get out of it? I felt like when you sit on a roller coaster and they put that bar down and tell you to put your hands and feet in. I knew I was done. There's no getting off once it's clicking up the fucking track. I was on for the ride, and it sucked! I hated it!

On the very first night of our marriage, just a few hours after we exchanged our vows, I found myself in bed, lying on my back, while she was next to me in what could be called an alcoholic coma. I felt a single tear roll down my cheek, and all I was thinking was, "Why the fuck did I just do this?"

Our marriage lasted nine years. The only thing that kept me in it that long was that I found out early in the first year of marriage that my wife was part lesbo and wanted to do threesomes with hot chicks.

Let me explain further.

My band and I were doing a gig at a shithole on Long Island, where my wife and a girl named Cindy worked. They were both bartenders. At some point after the gig, my wife came up to me and said, "Cindy wants to come home with us and watch us fuck."

"Check! Check please!" I could not get out of the bar fast enough!

At the time, I drove the company air-conditioning and heating van everywhere, because I didn't have my own. So, I was driving drunk in the company van with my wife and this girl, Cindy, who was now sitting on my wife's lap. I wanted to do a thousand miles an hour, but I was thinking to myself, "Don't speed! Don't get pulled over! I have to make this fantasy happen!"

Cindy was twenty-four and super hot. Kind of trashy, but I love white trash. Can't fuckin' beat trailer park trash with a halter top and shorts. So she and my wife started making out in the van and we finally got back to the house and had "community shower time." It was as good as I could have possibly dreamed.

I woke up the next day and asked Jennifer if everything was okay. She was like, "Oh yeah!" She said to me, "Some days I'm like seventy percent lesbian and other days ninety percent." Let's just say Cindy became a regular guest at the house until I got my radio gig in Boston.

Now that I was on the radio, I was starting to get some attention from girls, and Jennifer said, "You ever think we'll be able to do stuff like we did with Cindy again?" In my head, I was like, "Yep!" But with her, I truthfully tried playing it cool. "I don't know. Would you even be into that?" I told her. Meanwhile I got rock hard just thinking about it. Oddly enough it never happened in Boston. We'd go back to New York to visit family and friends and end up fucking Cindy.

When we got fired from Boston and ended up back in New York, I tried getting other girls and introducing them to Jennifer. Instead of her saying, "Hey, you think we can do this?" I was the one asking, "Hey, you still want to do that?"

There was an instance with a girl named Melinda who came into the studio and got completely naked. She was dancing around and I was like, "Oh my fucking God, this is exactly my type of girl!" Crazy, cute, pale, trashy, and just great. (Have I mentioned that I love white trash?) She was into me and I knew she wanted to do…*something*.

I took that beautiful nugget of information back home and let the wife know, "I finally met someone!" So I set something up for us at this gig I had to do, a huge Jersey Shore beach party. A very cool *O&A* event. She came with us, and the entire time my mind was just on landing Melinda and Jennifer. I had to make this fantasy happen! I was just obsessed!

I booked a room at the Plaza hotel in Manhattan, and we went there directly from Jersey and had a great sex romp. After that night, I started developing feelings for her. She was a very cool chick, and at this point I knew I hated my wife.

We started having these threesome liaisons regularly. Jennifer made it clear that there was never to be sex unless she was included. I said,

"Well of course, honey! We only fuck the same girl together! What am I, an animal?" There are rules with cheating.

This went on for about six months, with the three of us doing this once a week. Melinda didn't like my wife; she just wanted to hang out and have sex with me. You can always tell if your marriage is being destroyed by a threesome if you're with the other girl and your lovemaking looks like a scene out of *From Here to Eternity*. You're just rolling on the beach and having the most erotic lovemaking, but one hand is shoved out so your finger can diddle your wife at the same time. That's exactly what was happening.

Ironically, that's how Opie must have felt when Jim Norton and I were doing the show.

Toward the end of our relationship, Jennifer and I even started bringing Melinda out with Opie and his longtime girlfriend, Sandy Delgado. It wasn't an in-your-face, "look who's with us now!" kind of thing, but it was enough that Sandy was starting to get very pissed off and disgusted. Sandy started telling my wife to try to put an end to it. It was this symbiotic relationship with Team Opie, which included Sandy and Jennifer, conspiring to put an end to my relationship with Melinda. It was the circle of life, the balance of power all resting on everything being perfectly in sync, and the split second one of those Jenga logs came out, the whole fucking thing came tumbling down.

People were like, "You fucked up your marriage for the girl you had a threesome with?!" Hey, I ended up with Melinda for nine years, which ended up being the most devoted monogamous relationship I've ever had with a girl I cheated on my wife with. Melinda was probably the only girl I can say I truly loved.

And this relationship with Melinda was definitively the catalyst for the downfall of my relationship with Opie.

Melinda lived in NYC and would stop in to see me at the studio, and Opie fucking hated it. It was almost like he would go out of his way not to say hello to her, which I took as an insult. Opie wanted to confront me about this and talk about it, but he wasn't going to do it unless I brought it up. We were the worst possible combination of conflicted people.

I don't give a shit if there's bubbling lava around me, as long as what I'm standing on isn't lava, I'm fine. "Oh, the lava's approaching? It's gonna burn me at some point? I don't care. Right now, I'm great. Not a problem in the world." I was too much of a pacifist about the whole thing.

Until we had our first on-air argument, no one ever knew we had any problems. We could turn the microphones on and people would envy how we sounded together. They would never know that the minute the mics weren't on, we could be at each other's throats. I remember times off air when we'd be dispensing mutual fuck-yous and one second later starting the show like nothing ever happened. We were both pros.

That said, the stress and pressure of this animosity we had was insane and weighed heavily on us, but I was making more coin than I had ever dreamed of and wasn't gonna fuck that up. Always the show first!

Opie knew I was fucking around. The rule Jennifer and I had about not fucking anyone without each other went out the window. Melinda would come over to our house in Huntington and spend the weekend. We'd hang out and go to dinners and movies, drink, and then fuck at home.

My wife would get up in the morning and be like, "Okay, I'm going to take a shower." The second that bathroom door shut, I couldn't be on top of that girl fast enough to bang her without having to diddle my wife on the sidelines. It was so hot, and then she'd come out of the shower and we'd have to pretend we were watching television. "Oh, hey, you're back!"

Then my wife got a bug up her ass thinking that if we had kids, everything would be okay. She made a concerted effort to get pregnant, and I was like, "No fucking way." But again, I'm a diplomat and didn't want to get into a heated argument, so I would be fucking her and pretending I was coming. I'd put on the "I'm coming" face, thrust, and make the orgasm appear legitimate. Then I'd go into the bathroom and jerk off. I was so convincing, and it got so bad that she made us go to a fertility clinic. The doctor said, "You two are extremely fertile. I can't quite understand why this would be happening." Why? Because I was jerking off into the toilet.

Opie was hearing it every night from Sandy about what a piece of shit I was. I know he didn't want to get involved. No guy wants to hear about his friend having a threesome in a negative way, especially from his girlfriend. After a while it just pissed Opie off.

At this point, I wanted nothing to do with my wife anymore. After a while, my wife could tell what was up and wanted to put an end to it, and gave me an ultimatum. It was my best chance to just say, "Okay, bye!" And that's what I did. Fortunately, we divorced when I was making only about 145,000 dollars with WNEW FM, which at the time was un-fucking-believable money. A couple of years before, I had been making twenty-eight thousand dollars knocking tin with an air-conditioning company. This was right before we signed the next deal, which was *ludicrous* money.

A tipping point was a softball game at Bears stadium in Newark, New Jersey. It was a great *O&A* event, with a packed stadium of eight thousand people. Celebrity players, like Jay Mohr (who was huge at the time) and Tracy Morgan, were there with us. We had strippers behind home plate in a kiddie pool. It was just a debaucherously great fucking time! So my girlfriend, my girlfriend's sister, and her husband show up, and I wanted them to have carte blanche, all-access VIP passes that included the dugout and locker room.

Rick Delgado was our executive producer of the show and the brother of Opie's girlfriend, Sandy. Rick came up to me and said, "I'm sorry but they can't come in." I was like, "You're fucking shitting me, right?" Rick wasn't joking. "Opie just wants show people and the players in this area." I knew this was a direct jab at me and Melinda.

This was beyond ridiculous. I could bring whomever I wanted. If I wanted to get strangers from the stands and bring them into the dugout, I could. I confronted Opie and said, "This is bullshit!" We had a little discussion. It wasn't a heated argument, but it wasn't very pleasant. He pulled an "oh no, they're allowed down there." I told him there was no way Rick would ever tell me I couldn't bring someone anywhere unless he had been specifically told to do so by Opie. This was an example of Opie saying, "I'm not your boss *but* I'm your boss." The animosity was just escalating.

Occasionally we did talk about it. There was a time I was in Philly at my hotel and Melinda was just balling her eyes out, saying, "He fucking hates me. He doesn't say hi. Never introduces me to anyone and just ignores me!" *Now* I had to do something. She was crying in my hotel room, for Christ's sake. I took that opportunity to approach him and said, "Look, you need to change your attitude with Melinda. This isn't just the girl that busted up my marriage; I truly care about her, and you're completely disrespecting her and through that *me* by acting like this!"

He apologized and acknowledged it was hard to deal with this situation. That was the typical example of how he would put something off a little bit longer. After that, for a couple of weeks things would be great. I then realized there was a constant problem of there always being *something*.

Our job is quite possibly the easiest one you could have. "I command you to go into that room and talk with your friends, laugh, and don't come out for three or four hours." Wow! What a tough gig. If you've worked for a living and if you've been on a rooftop in August or an attic in July, you know what work really is. And to work in a studio and make jokes for a living is not fucking work. Some people don't know that working-class life, and I don't think Opie did. That was another part of our personalities that just didn't click.

CHAPTER 11

The Voyeur Bus

On November 30, 2000, our show on WNEW caught wind of a voyeur bus that was driving around Manhattan letting woman have the right to show their tits in public without being arrested.

We got in touch with this company and had them come down to our show to interview them. It was a half dozen girls, the guy who ran the business, and the driver. It was a Greyhound-style bus that had been converted into a makeshift motor home. The sides were clear glass, so anyone could easily see into the bus. Inside was a shower, bedroom, living room, workout facility, and of course a pole. This company featured nude or semi-nude models who could be followed on their nationwide bus tour via a paid website.

We knew this was right up our alley and something we wanted to get our names attached to for the great press. During the interview, we asked if we could send a few of the girls that were with us and some of the guys from our show to join them during their drive around the city. It was decided that it would be Jim Norton, Lewis Black, executive producer Rick Delgado, head of production Steve Carlesi, and the girls we had from the best-tit contest. Psycho Mark jumped in later during the ride. We all joined the girls who were already part of this bus crew.

We did remote breaks, with our guys calling in to tell us what the people outside were doing.

The remotes were fantastic! We traveled right down Broadway and through the heart of Times Square. ABC was showing David Blaine in a block-of-ice stunt he was doing, and he actually waved to the naked girls as they passed by. MTV had to change its camera angles because they were doing *MTV Total Request Live* with Carson Daly and he was caught checking out the girls. There were families on vacation and here was this bus with topless broads driving right by them for everyone to see. It became a real spectacle, and we were the ones orchestrating it.

The NYPD officers were such good friends with the show, they decided to give the bus an official police escort. They had two cop cars in front of the bus clearing the way so it could continue its route.

This whole thing turned into big news very quickly. We got a call from CNN correspondent Jeanne Moos, who asked if we could pick her up with a film crew. She said it sounded like it could be a fun segment for them to air. Hell yes! We obliged and picked them up prior to one of our stops, at City Hall. We had no idea what her real intentions were, which was to lambaste this whole thing. When we got to City Hall, Jeanne Moos said she had all that she needed and asked to be let out. That sneaky bitch went right into Mayor Giuliani's office to share with him the footage and rat us out.

Meanwhile, the bus was headed up Sixth Avenue back to our studio, and the police escort all of a sudden disappeared. There wasn't any traffic on the street at all. The bus was just moving along making all the lights, and out of nowhere and from everywhere came every type of law enforcement vehicle you would think existed. There were state police, NYPD, and black cars with no identification on them turning in front of the bus, stopping and pulling it over. Cops got out and dragged everyone off the bus immediately. The girls were able to put shirts on.

They wound up arresting everyone on the bus. Poor Lewis Black, a political comedian, had thought it would be fun to take a ride on the bus with some naked chicks and was sent along with everyone else downtown to "the Tombs" corrections facility. Things happen.

What we had failed to realize was that President Clinton was coming into New York City around that very time. He had already landed at Kennedy airport, and this part of Sixth Avenue had been blocked off for his arriving motorcade.

The voyeur bus of all things decided to make a turn onto Sixth Avenue and continue up until it was stopped.

The irony is that President Clinton would have gotten a kick out of a bus full of nude women. I could see him saying, "I really like this New York City welcome!"

Then we had to go through legal channels trying to get Jimmy, Lewis, Rick, Steve, and Psycho Mark out of jail. Mayor Giuliani did not like this at all. There was a press conference, and a reporter asked him, "What's your take on this voyeur-bus *Opie and Anthony* thing?" "Stupid. Just stupid." Which is another great quote I have from a man in a powerful position about our program.

I would assume it came from the top that "regardless of what you find or don't find, hold these motherfuckers for at least twenty-four hours. Just hold them and don't let them out." We couldn't find any lawyer to get these guys out of there. They were like, "What are they charged with?" "Well, we're still working on it and compiling charges."

All the men were placed together in a holding cell. The same with the women. After twelve hours, the guys were put into the general pop. They were now surrounded by hardcore criminals who would beat the shit out of you if you looked at them the wrong way. It's said that Jim Norton fit in like he had been cast for it. Twitching and talking to himself non-stop. No one even considered fucking with him. Poor Lewis Black didn't come back on our show for quite a while.

When all was said and done, twenty-eight hours later no charges had been filed. They went in front of the judge, and he was pissed he even had to waste his time with such nonsense and released them immediately.

We were again just millimeters away from being fired for that one. On days like that, you're either fired or they're patting you on the back and loving you because the ratings are huge. The new book would come out, and we'd be on the very top. This only made us look for something else to top ourselves. Maybe sex in a church? Maybe sex in the biggest Catholic Church in NYC or, arguably, the whole country? Yeah…

CHAPTER 12

Syndicated and Vindicated

I N 2001, OUR THREE-YEAR contract with WNEW was ending, and we started renegotiating a new deal. Clear Channel Communications came in with another offer for us to have our own morning show on Q104.3 to go up against Howard Stern.

Whether we beat Howard Stern or not was inconsequential. CBS knew that we could potentially take enough listeners away to keep him from being number one. This made us a commodity to CBS, and they did not want us to leave. Howard's number-one status in mornings made them billions of dollars. Howard needed to remain on top or they would lose a boatload of money, and there was a very good chance he would not be number one if we went against him. That was all the math they needed to say, "Write these fucks a giant check and give them what they want." We wanted syndication. We of course wanted to be back on the air in Boston. We had gotten thrown out of there and knew it would be legendary to come back on their airwaves. This was our General MacArthur-in-the-Philippines moment:

"I shall return!"

We ended up in eighteen cities. Washington, DC; Philadelphia; New Orleans; and Houston, to name a few. We played predominantly in East Coast cities because of the time delay and our starting at 3:00 p.m., which would be noon on the West Coast.

When we made the syndication deal, it was one of the most surreal moments I've ever experienced. Our agent, Bob Eatman, had a room in the Parker Meridien hotel in Manhattan and was fielding calls. Opie and I sat in the hotel room listening to his back-and-forth with Infinity Broadcasting/CBS, discussing the cities we would be broadcast in and the money amounts to go with it. We were getting a three-year contract, and each city had an annual salary. There would be bonuses according to ratings. The potential for money was amazing, and the actual money was ludicrous in the very best way. I was listening to Bob say these exorbitantly large numbers for our salaries and was looking at Opie like, "This can't be real. Did he really say that amount?" We were entering into the realm of "fuck-you" money.

Opie and I were just pacing and nervously laughing at times. Bob was repeating out loud the numbers they were offering us, so we could hear and it was millions of dollars.

Here I was a full-fledged shock jock and *I* was the one being shocked hearing these massive amounts of money being offered to us. I was numb. It was like one of those out-of-body experiences you hear about when someone gets close to dying and is floating outside of their own body. Was I dreaming? Was I going to wake up at any moment and be like, "Fuck, I knew it was too good to be true"? I was waiting for the building to collapse or something to mess this up. It was like having the hottest girl in the world come over to you and ask you to take her home and she really ends up fucking you. I couldn't believe I was going to be a multi-millionaire for doing something that was so much fun and easy to do. This was my dream coming true.

Bob got off the phone and ran through year one, year two, year three, all the cities our syndication deal came up with, and the bonuses.

There was no question of not signing this deal with CBS. Clear Channel just didn't have the number of stations and couldn't match the money. Clear Channel wanted us, but CBS wanted us more. Keep your friends close and your enemies closer.

We had a lot of crossover fans from Howard in the morning who listened to us in the afternoon. There were also a lot of dedicated fans in both camps who hated the other side. Even though we worked for the same company and our shows were on at different times, Howard saw us as competitors.

He would reference us as "my clones across the street." Howard knew we weren't just a couple of jocks he could squish like he did to so many others throughout the years. We didn't take shit, and we certainly didn't listen to our PD or GM on how we should handle Howard. We knew how to handle him. I had listened to him my whole life and knew exactly how to make people laugh at him. You can't just come into New York and say, "Howard sucks." The people would go, "What? No, he doesn't. He's great, I fucking love him."

We knew we could get away with doing impressions of him. Then people would be like, "Holy shit, that's funny." I was goofing on shit about Howard that I had known for years, and if someone heard that, they were like, "Fuck yeah, he really does do that." Howard always wanted his audience to see him as a regular guy. We would push it a funny way, telling people he was a Hamptons guy, part of the elite, and it chipped away at him. We kept doing that, and he knew it was effective and he hated it. Then he would retort by bashing us, and it wouldn't work because we were unconventional. We always found out when he was talking about us, and I'm positive he heard what we said too.

I don't know if Howard has any respect for me, our show, or any show other than his own. I have respect for him. He really was the first successful shock jock. There were other jocks before him who were kind of doing something. Howard was the one who wrapped it all up in a great package. One jock might have done bits, another was great at interviews, and this one was a little irreverent. Howard was able to put it all together seamlessly while surrounding himself with amazingly talented people. He became successful at the perfect time in the eighties and nineties, when radio was still king in your car and there weren't as many options. If you wanted something risqué or edgy, you listened to Howard Stern. Opie and I came in at the tail end of the shock jock thing. I think we're partially responsible for blowing up the whole genre as far as making headlines because of our outrageous antics.

We actually got in trouble internally because of Howard Stern. We became privy to some personal knowledge about Howard. He had a particular family situation of a very private nature. We alluded to it on the air in a very ambiguous way, and it got back to him. He was quite upset. This was literally right when we went on break for Christmas vacation. We got a call from Mel Karmazin's office to meet him at the Black Rock building in Midtown. We knew this wasn't a good thing. We had to wait in his lobby for at least an hour. I'm sure Mel told his secretary to let us sit there for a fucking hour.

When we finally walked into his office, he asked us, "What time do you wake up and decide you're going to fuck Mel Karmazin?" I was sitting there thinking, "This is one of those questions there's no answer for, is there?" You don't give him a time. It's not even a question about *if* you're gonna fuck Mel Karmazin. You've already fucked him. He just wants to know when you woke up and decided you were gonna do it. He said, "How does it do my company any good if my afternoon show is fucking my morning show? Should I go to my stockholders and tell them whatever you tell me about how it does the company good that you're fucking my morning show?"

You will never be smaller in a seat than when you're getting lambasted by Mel Karmazin. I was probably forty at the time, and I was getting yelled at by an adult. It brought me right back to when I was a kid getting yelled at by either my dad or a principal. I was waiting for him to call me "Pissy Eyes." The truth of the matter is that he had us dead to rights and we had nothing to say. The whole time I was just hoping not to hear "you're fired," and we didn't. I think we skated out of that one by a pube. Before we left, Mel gave us a stern warning letting us know that we were never to speak of Howard ever again. We walked out of there and let out a huge sigh. We felt this relief that we had made it out alive and been given another day. Then of course by the time we were a block away, we were like, "Fuck Stern, that fucking asshole!"

I had this pressure, like a piano hanging by a thread over my head, every fucking day. I just had to figure out how to tap dance to satisfy an audience and our bosses. I hoped this wasn't going to be the day the string would break and I'd get crushed. This was a constant thought. I felt this obligation to be better and bigger every show. I wanted to do better and be more outrageous every time, with the ratings constantly going up.

I wasn't even thinking about the financial bonuses. I just wanted to be able to say we had the best show and a fuck load of listeners loving it. To do this on a daily basis was pretty stressful. I was really balancing my entire job on keeping my job. It was very topsy-turvy, because if you're fired, that's it:

> *"Good luck on the next gig, maybe." Or it would be, "Oh my God, that was great! You're the best thing ever!"*

It's a fine line between those two things. We did that for so long, and it was exhausting.

In 2001, Vince McMahon and the WWF joined NBC to put together a professional football league called the XFL. It lasted one season, and games took place during the NFL's off-season. It was the extreme football league, with fewer rules and more violence.

One of the sports execs from NBC was tasked with the job of finding a pregame show for this new football league. Every football game has a pregame show that gets the viewers psyched up for the game they're about to see. NBC needed a couple of guys who could fill up the restaurant the WWF had in Times Square. It was a huge place with a big stage. They were going to be having the XFL cheerleaders and players.

They needed this place to be full and had to get a host who could draw a crowd in NYC. "Well, what about these guys Opie and Anthony? They could do it." "Yes, but do they know anything about television or hosting a pregame show? Do they even know anything about football?" "Fuck it, who cares as long as they can fill the place up?" That's my interpretation of what happened at 30 Rock.

Bob Eatman got approached and called us and said, "The XFL, which is this new pro football league, wants you both to host their pregame show." Opie and I immediately went, "No, that's not us. We're not those guys." "Oh, okay, I'll tell them." Bob came back again, saying, "Alright, here's their new offer. They really want you guys to do this," and again we refuse. The third time, they came back with so much money, there wasn't any reason we weren't gonna do this.

They wanted us to commit to one season, which would be thirteen hour-long episodes, and it was just hundreds of thousands of dollars. It was a lot of money. So finally, we were like, "Yeah, fuck it! Let's do this pregame show!" Totally for the money. We told them we had a radio show that was our priority and we didn't have the time to come up with an hour-long show each week. "You guys have the writers at NBC, so you'll have to be responsible for that end of it. Fair enough, right? You tell us what we need to do, and we'll do it." They say no problem, and we sign the contract. Done deal. We were now the hosts of the national weekly pregame show for the XFL.

Day one, the first show, we made our way to the WWF restaurant. They were like, "Alright, what are we doing?" We're like, "We don't know. We were planning on you telling us." "Well, we have the cheerleaders dancing over here, and Bruce Beck is going to be our NBC sports correspondent that you'll be throwing something to sometime during the hour. In between, you got any bits?" Bits? See, now Opie and I are expected to come up with shit every week to fill time in between the dancing cheerleaders and Bruce Beck doing analysis. I was in the kitchen of the cafe thinking, "What am I going to do?" I was working on dick jokes for national TV an hour before we were fucking gonna tape!

We received no support from NBC, and we knew it stank. We were up onstage with the cheerleaders and almost dancing. We're like, "We'll be right back," and we were standing with the dancing cheerleaders and it was so awkward.

These people who filled this vacuous restaurant were all *O&A* fans. They didn't know or give a shit about the XFL, and they just wanted to be entertained. They also wanted to entertain us in return. Their mindset was that they were part of the show. There were three cameras filming this show, and there were two guys in front of the stage. They decided they were going to get in our camera shot and with their hands pretend to be jerking off Opie and me as we were talking.

They were doing this the whole time we were onstage and no one caught it till editing. They couldn't use one wide shot for the entire segment. They wanted an audience, and we provided them one. We didn't promise anything about quality work. We had a female announcer introduce us on the show: "And now, Opie and Anthony!" You'd hear the audience chanting, "Show your tits!" The sound would get picked up and we'd have to cut and do it again. They'd come to the dressing room and go, "Um, guys, is there any way you can get your audience to stop saying, 'Show your tits?'" I said, "If we go out there and tell them to stop it, it's going to be twice as loud. You don't understand, we can't control these things." Mercifully, after four episodes the whole XFL thing was scrapped. That was it for the pregame show. They did have to pay us out for the whole contract, and I feel we earned every cent of it. XFL was the second-biggest disaster of 2001, and not by much.

CHAPTER 13

St. Patrick's Cathedral

WE HAD A RADIO contest that we knew would create a lot of attention. This wasn't the first time we had done it, but it ended up being the last. We promoted the contest months in advance and had all these couples audition, which we narrowed down to five. These couples would be accompanied by a chaperone to verify that they actually accomplished the tasks given to them. The chaperones included Rich Vos, Stephen Lynch, Ben Sparks, Rick Delgado, and of course Paul Mecurio, who became key in this story. The winner would get a trip to Boston to the Samuel Adams brewery for a beer-tasting tour and a Sox game.

For this Sex for Sam contest, the couples got a huge list of famous NYC landmarks to have sex in. The couple who had intercourse in five of these places and posted the highest score would win. The Empire State Building, F.A.O. Schwarz, Hard Rock Cafe, the Rockefeller building, and an ESPN van were a few of the places. At the bottom of the list, for this year only, Opie added a church. We had so many landmarks to choose from that adding a church to the list was almost just for a laugh. On the show that day when we announced the landmarks, we said it last. "Blah blah blah and a church." We never in a million years expected anyone to actually pick the church.

The chaperones would follow these contestants and would call in to the studio and make it sound like it was a sporting event. I'd be like, "Okay, we have Ben Sparks at the Empire State Building with a couple. Whattaya got, Ben?" "Well, we're here at the Empire State Building with the couple, and yes, they're doing it! They're doing it doggie style right now!"

We had a point system with certain bonuses. If the guy stuck his dick up her ass, the team was awarded a two-point conversion. The harder the location, the higher the point value. Central Park had a lower point value because it was easier to find a place to bang in than a church, which had the highest point value.

We took calls during the contest, and we got one from chaperone Paul Mecurio. Within a second he was telling us, "We're here at St. Patrick's Cathedral, and he's doing a two-point conversion."

Here's where we came to the radio conundrum that has haunted us for years upon years. Opie and I looked at each other knowing this was bad but this was also great radio. We knew that for listeners to hear he was fucking her in the ass at St. Patrick's Cathedral was great. As far as the people at the church, mayor's office, police department, and FCC and our bosses were concerned, it wasn't good.

So what do you opt for when you literally have seven seconds to hit that dump button?

Opie, Al Dukes (the guy down the hall in the locked room), and I all had the ability to hit this dump button that could have wiped out the call. This guy Al Dukes had been brought in from CBS because they didn't trust us and wanted a company guy there in case of something just like this. It was his job to make the executive decision about what wasn't appropriate for the airwaves. Ironically, he was the only one who came out of this unscathed. We could have hung up the phone and continued our lives as the *Opie and Anthony* show on WNEW.

No one hit the dump button. That was the mindset of what our radio show had become. I thought about it and looked at Opie, and he knew we had this option as well. All I knew was that this was more outrageous than what we had done the previous day, and we needed to be more outrageous every day.

We never hit that button, and then we kicked it into high gear. "Really? Paul, what's going on?" "Well, we're here by the front door, and he's pumping her really hard. Oh wait, there's someone coming over to us."

Now again, we could have said, "Run!" but we chose to get the play-by-play, asking, "Who's coming over?" We wanted that dialogue between whoever was coming over and Paul, who was going to attempt to justify this couple's having anal sex by the front door of the most highly regarded religious landmark in the United States.

"It was one of the security guards from St. Pat's." We were now listening to the back-and-forth between Paul and this security guard. The security guy was like, "What is going on here? Why are you two pulling up your pants?" "Oh no. Don't worry, it's just a radio contest."

Again, they could have left. The guard said, "I'm calling the cops." Paul and the couple should have hightailed it the fuck out of there. Paul was arguing with the guy because he'd been a regular on our show and we loved when he was confrontational on the phone. This wasn't his first rodeo for us. One time, Paul went to a Broadway show starring Kathleen Turner that was controversial because she took her top off during the play. Paul was sitting in the middle of the theater and was on the phone with our show. She was in the scene where she was going to take off her shirt, and he was telling us, "She's doing it now," and we heard him yell, "Hey, Kathleen, put your goddamn shirt back on!"

We could actually hear the gasp of horror from the audience. Then security came over to remove him from the theater. Paul demanded he get his money back, and they gave it to him.

Knowing we loved this from him, he kept it going with the security guard in St. Patrick's up until the police came. Once the cops came, all bets were off; there was no leaving. We were riding this whole thing out with him. We heard everything up until Paul was handcuffed. They arrested Paul and the couple—who, by the way, did get the highest points for one place but sadly didn't win the contest with their overall score.

Mind you, other than Paul, no one else had witnessed the sex act. The security guard only saw them pulling up their pants. At first, he thought they were defecating. They never ended up getting charged with anything and were released.

Nonetheless, it had already been put out there by the news that a couple had been caught fucking in St. Patrick's Cathedral. Then when people found out about it and we were being highlighted as the ones who had orchestrated this event, we knew it was going to be similar to our situation with the mayor of Boston.

Our first reaction was, "Here it is! *O and A* back in the news! We're outrageous!" Then some people started to become outraged. The Catholic League said, "Did you know that this particular day on the Catholic calendar has significance?" Three hundred sixty-five days and of course it's the day of something! They started really turning the screws on management.

We went on air the next day, and our final guest on WNEW was, of all people, Brian Regan, who happened to have been our first guest on this show. We went full circle, with Brian bringing us in and taking us out.

The story became national news and even became exaggerated. We heard people thinking Opie and I had fucked each other in the church! So crazy. In an ironic way, Opie did fuck me by coming up with the idea of adding that church to the list, and I didn't even get a two-point conversion for it.

Then once again they had an internal investigation and suspended us while they found out who else was involved so they could fire them also. About a week later Jim, Opie, and I, after having lunch, were walking toward Opie's apartment when Bob Eatman called us. Opie put him on speakerphone and Bob told us, "They canceled the show. Your show is canceled."

I was driving home to Brooklyn and saw this bus driver's pushed-up newspaper in the front window, and it said, "Opie and Dopey." I vividly remember saying out loud, "I'm Dopey?"

We had signed the three-year deal with WNEW not knowing that after a year our show would be off the air. We still would get paid millions for two full years without being allowed to work. They said, "Here's your contract, and we are holding you to it. We're canceling your show but still paying you in full, and you're not allowed to get another job. Have fun!" They knew we'd go right to Clear Channel and compete against Howard Stern. They kept us from working for two years.

It wasn't all bad news. When you see your bank account just grow exponentially every time you look at it and you know it's gonna be happening for two years without any responsibility, it's pure bliss. I could just pick up and fly anywhere in the world on a whim. It wasn't the healthiest lifestyle with the drinking, gambling, smoking, and no struc-ture or hours to be accounted for, with unlimited money. If I were a drug addict, I surely would have died.

Looking back, if there was ever an addiction Opie and I shared, it was that need to constantly top ourselves and make our show the most talked about. We wanted our ratings to always go up and our listeners to be rewarded daily with our insanity. It was inevitable that we were going to get fired from WNEW. The thread finally broke, and the piano crushed us.

CHAPTER 14

Limbo

INITIALLY THE HARD PART of being fired was trying to convince my family that everything was okay. I certainly didn't know or think it was. Opie and I were damaged goods and as fucked as you could possibly be in the radio biz. Even when our contract was up in two years, we might attract zero interest. I thought this time we really might have done it to ourselves to the point of no coming back.

We had fucked up bad, and it was frightening.

My family had been so proud and amazed at what I had accomplished in this industry. It went from their seeing me as a completely irresponsible employee in the real working world to their knowing I was a multimillionaire radio personality. Prior to this success, I had been the one in the family everyone was constantly worrying about. "Is Ant going to be able to pay his rent?" It wouldn't have been a stretch for me to be knocking on their door asking for a place to sleep. I was that guy. To have transcended from that to what we accomplished in Boston and then New York was beyond anything my family or I ever could have imagined.

It wasn't like I had the luxury of hiding my firing. I was on the cover of the newspaper as half of "Opie and Dopie" and had to reassure my family that this was just part of the business. That I been through this before and would totally get another radio gig. I didn't even know if I could put it across believably because I didn't believe it when I was saying it, but it was important for me to put them all at ease.

The worst part of our being fired was not being able to get another job for the duration of two years. That's a long time not to work and to be so far removed from our fans.

I was still getting paid and had all this money pouring in with twenty-four hours in a day to fill by doing nothing. I started realizing how important structure was and having something to do except spending insane amounts of money to entertain myself. I found it hard trying to fill my day. On paper it sounds great, having a ton of money and nothing to do with zero responsibility.

During this time, I was living with my girlfriend, Melinda, in Brooklyn on Shore Road. Melinda was the bright side in all of this. We were having fun and would travel together. We vacationed at the opulent Atlantis hotel in the Bahamas for two weeks. As we were checking out I said, "What are we going to do when we get home?" She was like, "I don't know." We were rolling our luggage past the front desk and I said, "Ya know what? Can we get our room for another two weeks?" We went right back upstairs and stayed a month at the resort.

It's difficult not to have the mindset of someone who has something to do. "It's been two weeks and…" but there's nothing after "and."

We traveled to California. I bought a radio-controlled helicopter, because I'd read an article about one and was like, "Yep, I'll get that. That'll be a hobby for a few months." I've always had a love of rifles and shooting since I was a boy. I currently have a New York state and city pistol permit and carry a gun everywhere I go. The fun and sportsman-ship of shooting is amazing. I'm not a hunter. I understand people who are and hold nothing against them. I just always felt bad. You shoot something that was hopping around a moment before and now is gone. I'd rather shoot at targets without the guilt.

I like all types of guns and rifles. I own a Barrett fifty-caliber that you can shoot from a mile away and take someone's fucking head off. They're just fun to shoot. I don't care how much of a liberal someone is, the second they hold that stock against their shoulder and pull that trigger, an unbelievable explosion happens. The pressure changes around you, and you feel like you have the flu for three seconds. Then you start laughing your ass off. It's one of those primal things men just like, and I've always been fascinated with it. My father always had guns, and he taught me at a very young age how to shoot. Safety was always paramount. I just enjoy guns and, of course, like the idea of being able to protect myself. I've been called paranoid and heard people say, "You must have a small dick if you need a gun." Well, not if the other person has one! Read the news. Shit does happen.

I'd rather be on even footing with whoever my potential assailant is. I don't want to get into a knife fight with a guy or a fist fight with someone who is two times my size. I'm certainly extremely level-headed. I'm not the type of person rolling down my car window and saying, "I'll put a cap in your ass, motherfucker!" I am the type of person who, when someone rolls down their window and says that to me, will be able to retort, "No you won't, motherfucker!" So, guns, traveling, and a remote-controlled helicopter helped keep me busy. You can only bang your girlfriend and jerk off so many times.

If I had been fired from a job I hated, this would have been a dream come true. "You mean I don't have to go to work, but I still get paid the same amount as if I did? I don't have to go into an attic with insulation? I don't have to cut a hole out of the rooftop, and I'm still going to get paid?" But it was different, because I had been doing radio and it was the greatest job in the world.

Radio was something I relished doing. I loved the fans, the notoriety, and the compliments from people walking down the street. Knowing every day that passed was yet another day the fans wouldn't hear me on air was excruciating. I wasn't even 100 percent sure there was going to be a next time. The last thing I wanted to be was a non-issue, irrelevant, and someone who wasn't in the game anymore.

We were in our prime and never more popular when this transpired. It sucks to not be working in any phase of a gig you love. Not to work at the height of our popularity when we were at the top of our game was torture. No matter how much fun I had spending my money, I always felt I'd rather be working for it.

Aside from the divorce and Melinda, this firing was instrumental in the deteriorating relationship Opie and I began to have. We didn't have that constant daily contact anymore. We couldn't relate to a lot of things the other person did as an individual without radio being the central bonding point. Opie went out to some of Jim Norton's gigs during this time. Oddly enough, Opie and Jimmy were closer than I was with either of them. I was the one who was cut off and alone. That didn't bother me in the least. I had Melinda and was more than content.

I just missed the working element. It was a void that nothing could fill in my heart. And my health had deteriorated so badly that at the ripe old age of forty-two, I had to have a stent put in. All the drinking, smoking, and eating fast food while using the minimal amount of movement playing video games had taken its toll. I had pains in my chest. I was like, "This isn't normal," and got it checked out. They told me I needed a stent procedure. I decided to quit smoking and give up fast food. I still needed to drink, gamble, and play video games. I'm only human, for Christ's sake!

Seriously, this was a life-changing time when I realized I needed to work out and eat more healthfully. It wasn't like I was training for a triathlon. I just didn't want to be found dead with a controller in my hand, in front of my TV, and have people think, "Wow, he really took Call of Duty seriously!"

CHAPTER 15

XM—A Second Chance

W E TRIED HAVING OUR agent, Bob Eatman, negotiate our return: "Can we settle this to where you pay them a percentage and allow them to work? Can we get them out of their contract?" We were willing to take less money! We said, "Look, give us half of it and then we'll just go to work." We knew we could make that money working somewhere else and that getting back on the air was the most important thing to both of us. They didn't budge and wouldn't let us out of our deal. It was legal for Bob to start talking to other companies a few months before the contract expired. CBS had the choice to match whatever someone else offered, but they wanted nothing to do with us anymore. The people at Clear Channel had changed management, and we weren't an option.

We were damaged goods, and FM radio wanted to keep its distance as well. Bob came to us and said, "Hey, guys, I talked with the people at XM Satellite Radio," to which our initial reaction was, "Aww, fuck!" Satellite radio was radio jail. It was where everyone who couldn't be on regular radio went. Whether it was for lack of talent or being persona non grata, it was not the first place you'd want to go as a radio personality. FM was the place you wanted to be.

Nonetheless, this relatively new entertainment medium was our only option. There were two satellite companies: XM and Sirius. They were completely separate entities back then. Sirius was more like regular FM radio. They played mostly music and had regular jocks spinning tunes.

XM was weirder and eclectic. They wanted it to be what radio wasn't. They wanted to transcend FM radio and not do the same hacky bits. You'll never hear a top-five-hundred countdown on the Fourth of July. They wanted to do different things with broadcasting and saw this as the future of radio.

Bob was negotiating with both Sirius and XM to drive up our money. All of a sudden, for unknown reasons, Sirius cut us off and never spoke to us again. We asked Bob, "What's going on? What happened?" He said he didn't know. Then it was announced that Howard Stern was going to Sirius. We just couldn't get away from this fucking guy! We had two companies bidding on us and in came Howard. Sirius was no longer an option. They nabbed the best guy in the business.

That left us with XM and doing morning shows competing against Howard. We signed the contract on August 3, 2004, at XM headquarters in Washington, DC, followed by a public announcement and press conference at the Hard Rock Cafe two days later. Our first official show was planned for October 4. We knew we wouldn't be reaching the same number of listeners we had been accustomed to on terrestrial FM radio. We went from millions of listeners to a step up from those militant black Hebrew Israelites screaming into a bullhorn in Times Square. Even if we had the entire XM audience listening to us all at once, it wouldn't equate to even a tenth of what we had when we were syndicated on FM radio. The reality is, we couldn't get to everyone. Realistically speaking, we were probably talking to fewer than twenty thousand people a day, which was very depressing.

When we first got to XM, they wanted to brand us with our own channel. We wanted a good name, something that represented us and the type of show our fans expected. Unbeknownst to us, XM had already decided to label our channel High Voltage. High Voltage? It was ridiculous, and after our first contract negotiation, our first order of business was to change the name. We went with The Virus, because once we got on the air, we would be contagious and eat away at the competition.

We were doing the morning drive, which just killed me. The last thing I wanted to do was wake up and do morning radio. I'm an afternoon guy. I started second-guessing myself, wondering if I could even do radio without having a few beers. I don't think I'd ever done radio without drinking. But I knew there was no way I was going to start sipping brews at 6:00 a.m. after my wake-up call with the stent procedure. That wasn't an option.

It's weird how I questioned if I could be entertaining without the social lubricant of alcohol. Thank God it worked out. Who knew? I was pretty successful without drinking on a daily basis. Miracles do happen.

XM was very supportive of the show and built us our very own beautiful state-of-the-art studio on 57th Street between Sixth and Seventh Avenues, which also happened to be on top of the old Steinway piano showroom.

A frequent guest on the show in those days was a comic named John Valby, aka "Dr. Dirty." He'd come in with a little Casio keyboard and play at the console. He saw our new studio for the first time and was like, "Wow, the Steinway showroom is downstairs! It's beautiful!" We came up with the idea for one of our producers to take him downstairs. It's fucking Steinway pianos. The showroom was the stuffiest, most pretentious environment in Manhattan, with all those gorgeous million-dollar pianos.

Valby is a classically trained pianist who is a virtuoso on the keys. We took him downstairs with a microphone and had him talk to one of the salespeople at Steinway. John looked like a homeless person and smelled like one. The salesman was feeling him out: "Do you play? How many years?" He didn't know John from a hole in the wall. John sat down and there were three employees along with the store manager watching him. He began playing this beautiful classical concerto, transitioning into some honky-tonk and ragtime music.

We were listening, and our producer had an earpiece and could hear the show with us, talking while John was performing. John then went into his comedy act, which consisted of extremely vulgar song parodies. He started singing, "I was out on a date in my daddy's car, I picked her up in a Manhattan bar. I finger-fucked her clit, I had my cock in her throat too deep, I was pumping her face, my pecker started to spit, the doctor said the bitch had an epileptic fit. Where oh where can my pecker be?"

The Steinway people were not laughing and were completely appalled. We asked if he could play one more quick one before they called the police, and he did a parody of "My Favorite Things" that went like this: "Blow jobs and hand jobs and eating clitoris, watching your grandmother douche at church service, brown pubic cunt hairs and toilet bowl rings, these are a few of my favorite things." Mission accomplished.

This was the essence of our show: find what's around us and go for it. Don't worry about trouble or Steinway calling our boss. That never entered our minds. Do it and if you get in trouble, try to find a way out of it.

Because Howard Stern left 92.3 K-Rock for Sirius radio, K-Rock needed a new morning show. They replaced Howard with David Lee Roth, the former lead singer of Van Halen. David had been a guest on Howard's show from time to time and told some entertaining stories. David talks a mile a minute. Howard had the talent to rein him in. If you're a good interviewee, then your interviewer is part of that. They know when to tell you to shut the fuck up and move on to another story. Without that kind of governor micromanaging him, David Lee Roth might be one of the worst people ever on radio. Nonstop rambling about eighteen different topics at a time and then throwing in a "bozzie bozzie bop!" Just awful radio, and they fired him faster than you can say "Sammy Hagar."

CBS went from making huge amounts of money with Howard to making nothing with David Lee Roth. Here's where money comes in. The same company that had fired us for the Sex for Sam contest and kept us on the payroll for two years while not letting us work for anyone else hired us back!

It was announced on April 24, 2006, that we were now taking over Howard Stern's old stomping grounds and doing the morning show on K-Rock. We had just signed the contract with XM for the morning show, and K-Rock said, "Let's work out some kind of deal where you can do both." So we were on K-Rock and XM simultaneously. Now obviously satellite is unrestricted, and K-Rock had to adhere to FCC rules. This meant that for the first three hours of our show, we couldn't curse or talk graphically about sex or any other controversial topic. At 9:00 a.m. we walked over to the studio that XM had built for us and did our uncensored show till 11:00 a.m.

The walk between studios was just a few blocks, and we had to decide what we were going to do during the length of time it took to make that walk. We came up with the idea of taking a shopping cart with a microwave transmitter battery pack and broadcasting our walk on the way over to the XM studio. We had mics, and our guests walked with us on 57th Street in Manhattan. It became a really cool part of the show that was the catalyst for some really funny bits that our paid subscribers were able to enjoy.

We'd have a gag in which Rich Vos would go into the restaurant Rue 57 with a microphone and just started doing his act for the patrons eating breakfast. They were like, "What the fuck is this guy doing?" And we'd have Jim Norton buy hardcore gay pornography from the magazine stands on 57th Street and pose questions to the street vendor and other customers. We would talk to the homeless. Opie is still in trouble with people to this day because of what he did to one homeless guy, Andrew, who offered us a piece of his cake. Opie just stomped on it with his foot. The poor guy was just sitting there saying, "I paid for that cake. I earned that cake." Opie didn't give a shit as long as it was good radio.

The great thing is that the listeners got to join us every day for a different adventure on this walk. Sometimes our fans would wait outside the building for us to come out and would walk with us. We'd have anywhere from ten to fifty people following us down the street. If we were talking to a homeless guy, they'd throw money to the dude. It was like a windfall for these people.

One of our funniest bits was with the comedian Patrice O'Neal. We called it "Nigger vs. Nazi." During this time period, the actor Danny Glover had made his plight known publicly that he couldn't get a cab in NYC because he was African American. Patrice was on the show and we were talking about it, and he said, "Yeah, nobody wants to pick up a nigger." I was like, "Hey, I have a Nazi helmet. I'll put it on and you stand upstream from me. We'll both try to hail a cab to see if the cab driver picks up a nigger or a Nazi." The first cab blatantly passed by Patrice and stopped for me. Patrice screamed, "Nazi! Nazi! You pick up a

Nazi over a nigger? You motherfucker! You didn't stop for a nigger! You picked up a goddamn Nazi over a nigger! You chose a Nazi brother!" The second cab stopped for Patrice. The third cab hedged its bets and went between us. The next one went for the Nazi. Patrice said, "I'm gonna pull this out for niggers!" Then Patrice tied it up and it was going to game seven. The deciding cab passed right by Patrice and stopped in front of me. I thanked him for picking a Nazi over an African American. The Nazis won. Crazy shit!

In 2006, our show did a comedy tour called "The Virus Comedy Tour." This was for all of our huge market cities, like New York, Boston, Cleveland, and Philly. The tour included Otto & George, Patrice O'Neal, Rich Vos, Louis C.K., Bob Kelly, and Bob Saget. We also sprinkled in other comics throughout the tour, including Ralphie May, Tracy Morgan, Frank Caliendo, Joe Rogan, Jim Breuer, Carlos Mencia, Dom Irrera, and of course Bill Burr.

Any other audience would have just sat, listened, and laughed. Our audience was composed of a bunch of maniacs. This wasn't a normal comedy show. It wasn't like there was a show at 8:00 p.m. and they'd get there an hour before, watch the show, and leave. We had stuff going on all day prior to the show as a buildup. There was a pest-petting pen where we'd have "Stalker Patti" along with "Big A," corralled off in hay and you could feed them, plus dunking booths and other sideshows to entertain our fans. It was an event filled with freaks and debauchery.

We had passionate fans who were really into it, and they knew how we treated each other on the show—comics constantly busting each other's balls. We brought the audience into what we were doing; they genuinely felt like they were part of it. The only negative to this was that they felt they were also part of the stand-up show. They felt entitled to heckle the comics unmercifully, which sometimes made the shows a fucking nightmare. We'd take the bad with the good and the good with the bad. It happened, and we understood it. They were enjoying themselves, so be it.

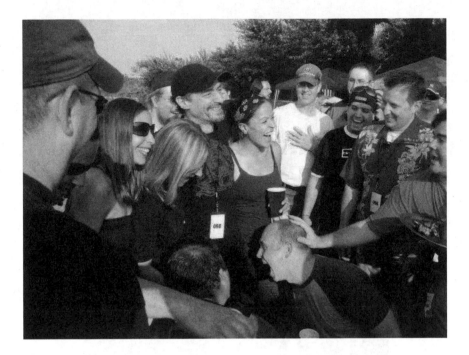

Our third show of the tour was in Philadelphia, and Philly is just notorious for being ruthless. Everyone is well aware of the Eagles fans who threw fucking snowballs at Santa Claus! Philly's own Dom Irrera was booed off the stage. It was brutal. Dom just disappeared. He was shell-shocked. Next up was Bill Burr. There was a digital clock facing the comic that would count down their time onstage. I think the sets were fifteen minutes long. Bill got huge applause when he walked onto the stage, and the clock started ticking down. Almost immediately after the applause, they started booing and yelling shit at him. Bill wasn't going to take it. "Really? Really?" Bill just started lambasting the crowd with a history lesson of Philadelphia and the inadequacies of Philadelphians. This guy knew everything there was to know about Philly. I defy a historian to know as much as Bill Burr knew that night about the City of Brotherly Love. He destroyed them. He referenced pop culture, sports, personalities, and the fucking Revolutionary War! Everything he brought up was a twist of the knife screwing Philadelphia, and the audience loved it. He told them:

> *"I wish you'd all die and the Eagles never win a fucking Super Bowl. Fuck all you motherfuckers and fuck the Flyers. Booing Dom Irrera? You can all suck my dick! What do you want me to talk about? Heart disease? I'm going to go to all of your funerals, and it's gonna be great."*

He started getting the audience to listen and laugh. He started counting down the show: "Eleven more minutes of this. Terrorists will never bomb you people, because the terrorists know you're worthless and nobody cares about you. You are this high above New Orleans. FEMA would never show up for you assholes!" He would keep counting down the clock in between disparaging comments about the audience and Philadelphia.

Bill waged war against this audience and made the impossible possible. He turned them! They went from booing to cheering and applauding. When he got done, he threw the mic down and received a full standing ovation. He won them over and actually got national recognition for it. This was a career moment for Bill. Unfortunately, the next gig was in Cleveland and they thought that Bill could re-create that with them. Bill was like, "Fuck that." He didn't know anything about Cleveland. What was he supposed to do, walk around with an encyclopedia about each city we'd perform in? He wanted to nip that in the bud, and he did.

XM was a completely different animal because it was uncensored. All the things we had to adhere to with the FCC on FM radio were thrown out the window. Saying "fuck" in front of a microphone was the weirdest thing. I'd say it and be like, "Oh no! Hit the dump button!" I had gotten used to doing radio without cursing most of the time. Sometimes it fits and it's great to throw a "fuck" or "shit" out there. When I'm telling a story, I'd rather spin it in a way that I don't have to just blurt out the seven dirty words. It was a new feel for radio. We could describe sex and bodily functions without corporate lawyers getting on us.

Race and being politically correct were always issues, even on satellite radio. Even though we were on a censor-free network that wanted to be cutting edge, we still almost got fired right away. I'm talking right the fuck out of the starting gate. Leave it to Opie and Anthony to push the parameters on a censor-free network their first couple of months working.

There was this funny homeless guy down the street from our studio who would talk all this outrageous shit. We decided to give this impoverished man a voice and let this batshit crazy guy get in front of our microphone. We brought him up to our studio and let him talk. He was actually pretty sharp and had some ideas—one of which was that he wanted to rape first lady Laura Bush. He also wanted to rape the queen of England and Condoleezza Rice. We were just laughing our asses off at the whole thing and how crazy he was.

We got done with the show feeling good about it. Then we started getting phone calls: "People are getting concerned. We're getting complaints, and the bosses here are a little upset about it." "What? This is satellite radio. This is absolutely what should be going out over their digital airwaves." The bosses said, "Something about raping Condoleezza Rice and you're all laughing." Then we heard from Reverend Al Sharpton. "Oh fuck!" This was the guy who got Imus fired for saying "nappy-headed hos." People took this guy seriously and were afraid of him. The bosses didn't want boycotts or anything else negative that could be stirred up. XM is a public company that needs investors and subscribers.

Once again, we were called onto the carpet to speak to the big bosses. I couldn't even believe it was happening. Déjà vu in the worst way. On May 15, 2007, it was announced that we were suspended for thirty days from satellite radio for content. The medium that had been professing freedom of speech, no restrictions, and anything goes suspended *Opie and Anthony* a month for content. Only us! Ironically, we didn't get suspended from K-Rock.

However, almost two years later, in March 2009, K-Rock decided to change to a dance music format, and then we just went full time at XM. Our last show at K-Rock was March 9. No one had told us this was going to be our last day. One of our producers, Erik Nagel ("E-Rock") found out through a back channel that the company was going to remove us, so we decided to make this our last show, and we announced it. We enjoyed our run while it lasted on K-Rock. It was a cool vibe and fun having

Howard's spot in his old studio. The fishbowl that Robin had sat in was still there. We had some really great, funny shows at that station.

XM began heating up with some personal conflicts. I think Opie had a lot of resentment for the business at that time. We were relegated to a medium that didn't have a lot of listeners. I don't know if he felt guilty about our getting fired, but we started understanding what satellite was about and what we could do to start getting back into being the *Opie and Anthony* show.

We wanted to get back to doing things like the Wiffle Ball Bat Challenge. We'd take a Wiffle ball bat, and if a girl wanted to try to win, we would put it up her vagina. Then we'd mark it with a Sharpie and measure it.

At the end of the year, the girl who got closest to the middle of the bat would win. Wholesome family fun, right? The bit itself was great. We would treat the bat like it was a priceless antiquity waiting to be auctioned off at Sotheby's: "Next is a Wiffle ball bat that women would stick up their twats on the *O and A* show. We'll start the bidding at twenty dollars." The coveted bat would be displayed in a glass case in our studio. We would always play holy music when taking it out when a girl came to compete. This was okay to do on satellite radio at the time. It was race that was the sticky wicket and frowned upon. Sex was completely fine.

We'd have girls get completely naked in the studio and perform sexual acts. We had a porn star come in and blow one of our producers in front of everybody. Hey, say what you want, but chicks getting naked and doing crazy shit is always fun.

This was when my eyes starting roving. Technology was improving with computers, video conferencing, and a thing called Paltalk, which I used to communicate with the fans. I would get video feeds of people and sometimes a good joke would come in, or I'd get stuck on discussing a movie and someone would provide me the answer. It was also good for watching girls in bed. Girls would put cameras of themselves in bed while listening to the show and be there with their tits hanging out. I got to know them through this and then got to know them better by actually hooking up with them. I was hooking up left and right with these chicks thanks to this video conferencing technology.

Opie started getting mad at me for this. He felt I wasn't paying enough attention to the show whenever I was looking down at the computer monitor. Well okay, "Ya got me!" This was the slow buildup to our having more problems. He at this point was with his fiancée, whom he did end up marrying and is still married to today. He wasn't looking for girls anymore, so of course enjoyed cock-blocking me whenever he could. In Opie's mind, Jim Norton and I were dogs. We were always on the hunt looking for a new conquest.

CHAPTER 16

Late-Night Dreams

XM RADIO DECIDED THEY REALLY wanted to promote our show, which included getting us on nationally televised talk shows. One of those was *Late Show with David Letterman*.

Our agent called us up and said, "Hey, you guys are doing David Letterman!" This was a week before the taping date, August 31, 2006.

Our reaction was as expected: "Holy shit! This is fucking amazing!" I had fantasized about this for years. I've watched every talk show since I was a kid. I loved Dick Cavett, Merv Griffin, Mike Douglas, and Johnny Carson. I would watch thinking, "This is the utmost coolest thing anyone could do, and I would love for this to happen to me at some point." I never actually thought it would. I would think about what exactly it would be like and run different scenarios in my head.

When we became syndicated and were becoming hugely popular, I started thinking it was a possibility that my dream could come to fruition. Knowing that there was the remotest chance gave me anxiety.

The news about Letterman was the scariest fucking thing I'd ever been told. I thought, "I'll step out on that stage and drop dead. It will be the first time that someone drops dead walking out to do a talk show. It's going to be all over the news that Anthony Cumia died walking on as a guest on Letterman." I couldn't handle my nerves even thinking about it. This nervousness lasted from the moment I found out till I was standing in the wings waiting to be announced to walk out. Every second of the day, I was consumed with, "Oh my God, I'm going to be on David Letterman and I'm going to drop dead on the stage. If I don't drop dead, I'm not going to do well. I'm going to freeze and not live up to the fantasy I've built up in my head."

The day arrived, and they picked Opie and me up in a limo to escort us to the Ed Sullivan Theater. A bunch of our fans were there waiting for our arrival at the back door where guests enter. They had it gated off, but our fans were waiting. There were girls asking us to sign their tits as we were walking into the place. We decided we were just gonna throw money into the crowd. We each had a giant stack of one-dollar bills, and just handed them out like we were giving back change from a grocery store. We made our way into the backstage area of the theater for makeup and hair. Then we went into the green room and I told Keith the cop, "I need beers back there." I had to down a couple of beers immediately to loosen up a little, or I was gonna lose my fucking mind. Keith came through, and I downed two beers instantly before the show. I had that nice slam-two-beers buzz.

Opie and I had a discussion about who was going to sit next to Dave. Obviously, I wanted to sit in the chair closest to Letterman. I didn't want to sit on the couch. Opie was clueless. I suggested we had to think about the audience's perspective. If they thought they were seeing Opie and Anthony from left to right, then I needed to be next to Dave. Opie agreed: "Okay."

He bought it, hook, line, and sinker! I don't know whether he was scared shitless to sit next to Dave. At this point, as nervous as I was, I knew damn well I needed to sit there. If this appearance was going to go well, I would have to take control of it and Opie would have to play second fiddle.

The producer walked us to the wings of the stage entranceway and held us off till it was time for our segment.

Meanwhile they were doing a bit in which they drop at least a hundred tennis balls from the ceiling onto the stage. So in between where we were in the wings and the first seat were at least a hundred tennis balls. I was looking at this and thinking, "I'm going to fall on my ass! There's no way I'm making it to my fucking seat." I had already been nervous enough about just walking out and dying of my own accord. Now I literally had to watch my footing to keep from tripping and cracking my head open. This had to be God's personal vendetta.

Then the segment producer told us to get ready, and we could hear from the wings, "From CBS Radio and XM Satellite Radio, from the *Opie and Anthony* show, please help me welcome Opie and Anthony."

We were walking out and I was kicking the tennis balls out of the way. I was looking at the audience, and it was un-fucking-believable. It felt like I was in a dream, and it was beyond surreal.

I made my way over to the big chair, and you can see on the video that I actually put my hand on the armrest and said, "This is it." I couldn't believe I was sitting on this fucking chair as a guest on David Letterman's show!

He asked us, "How are you two doing?" I couldn't even tell you after we finished what I had said or what had happened. It went by in a flash.

I do know that my mouth didn't stop moving the entire time. I was spitting shit out and just knew I had to keep talking. Opie laughed a little and tried to get his voice heard, but I was stomping on him. I knew his shit would suck. We were on national television, and it wasn't the time to be nice. I needed a guy who could be concise, telling a funny story, and that wasn't him.

Letterman started off the interview by going over the logistics of working on both terrestrial and satellite radio and how we worked it. Then he went into how we'd been fired a few times, and the audience just erupted into applause, and we briefly discussed the Mayor Menino story.

Dave asked if there were some ill feelings toward Howard. I quickly responded, "Yeah, there's this personal…I guess you'd call it hatred." Once again, the audience responded with applause. Howard had been on Letterman so many times, having great appearances and very funny shows. I realized I could do my Howard impression. I went right into channeling Howard sarcastically saying how he invented everything: "People stood there, and I invented locomotive walking. I invented breathing, Robin." I'm paraphrasing but my impression was dead-on and well received.

It seemed like Dave was looking for me to acknowledge Howard's greatness and also to see if there was room for us to reconcile our differences. I said, "Maybe in heaven?" and let everyone know that he had tried to get to us with our mutual bosses instead of going toe-to-toe with us on air. I added the hypocrisy of Mr. Free Speech's trying to stifle what we had to say about him. I then did another impression of Howard inventing Morse code, and even Dave cracked up at that one.

Dave clearly showed his loyalty to Howard by ending the interview with making us acknowledge that Howard had changed radio culture, to which I replied, "Yes he did." Then I added, "Yes, Senator, he did."

When I watched it later, knowing how scared shitless I was, surprisingly I looked comfortable and professional and did a great job. Meanwhile, I was doing an impression of every guest I had ever seen on a talk show my whole life. I was doing what I'd seen countless other guests do and making it my own. I even did the lean-over to Dave when our segment was over, pretending to have something to say to him. Ya gotta do the lean-over!

Opie and I walked back to our dressing room, and our entourage met us with smiling faces: Bob Eatman, Keith, "Club Soda" Kenny, and our significant others at the time. They were all congratulatory, telling us how well we had done.

After the show, we all went out for a celebratory dinner. I'd say about an hour into it, someone said, "Hey, pretty hard to shut Anthony up, huh?" That was the first inkling of someone's stating what the reality of the situation was. Everyone laughed, and I said, "I didn't know, I was just talking."

Opie was very quiet. I don't think he was mad. I think he knew he couldn't have handled that as well and was disappointed that he didn't get a chance to be more involved. I think he was smart enough to realize that my success was his as well.

I say this because when we later did *The Tonight Show with Jay Leno*, he didn't change anything. His attitude wasn't, "Let me sit next to Jay this time and talk more!" I think he knew I was the one who was going to move the interview and get the best result for us.

When we did Leno, they flew us out first class and put us up in a great hotel. Again, I was nervous as hell but at least had Letterman under my belt. I wasn't as freaked out and didn't think I'd drop dead on the stage walking out.

It was a different vibe from *Late Show*, which is right in the heart of Midtown Manhattan. *The Tonight Show* is in Burbank, California, and they have this huge NBC production facility. Jay actually introduced himself to us backstage prior to going on. He wasn't wearing his suit at the time. He was wearing denim with fresh oil stains, probably from working on one of the thousand cars that he owns. He was just a super nice guy. He gave us a killer intro as hosting the most popular radio show in the country: "They're syndicated and able to be heard all throughout the United States and also on XM Satellite Radio. Please help me welcome Opie and Anthony!" This time there wasn't a tennis ball obstacle course between the wings and our seats.

Matthew McConaughey was the guest prior to us, and he stayed on for our segment. He just slid over on the couch and Opie sat next to him and I took the spot right next to Jay. It was similar to our interview with Dave. He mentioned that we had a knack for being fired. It's really funny to talk about what you get fired for and how, especially on national television. Maybe it's schadenfreude? For some reason people find it hilarious. Opie did talk this time about running into Ron Howard at Starbucks, and it went absolutely nowhere. I was chomping at the bit, giving it three more seconds before I would jump in. I fortunately was able to resuscitate his story by getting the only laugh out of it.

Jay led me into some of my impressions, which included one of him, Tony Danza, and yes, Howard Stern, which earned me huge applause.

We mentioned the church incident, which confused Matthew McConaughey. He said, "You two had sex in a church?" It brought the house down and ended our segment.

At the very end of the show, Jay had a chainsaw-powered blender on his desk and made us all margaritas. We walked out onto the stage to say goodnight with our cocktails in hand. I looked out at the audience of *The Tonight Show*, once again not believing that this was my life.

Two of the greatest moments I've ever experienced in my professional life were being a guest on these iconic late-night shows.

CHAPTER 17

Bye-Bye, Melinda

Most loyal listeners know I love playing blackjack and going to the Borgata in Atlantic City. It's one of my favorite things to do. I would bring a little entourage with me that included Keith the cop, some of the guys I worked with at XM, friends, and Melinda.

We'd go down for the weekend, and they always provided me a great suite to stay in—which they should have, considering I'd sometimes play thirty grand a hand in the high-limit section. One particular night I had three six-thousand-dollar bets up on the table. I was completely engrossed in the game, and one of the waitresses came over.

The service you get at the high-rollers' table is exemplary. The second your drink gets a little empty, a Borgata babe comes over. These girls are the epitome of beautiful cocktail waitresses. You go to other casinos in Atlantic City and you're like, "Can I have another drink, Nana?" Some seventy-year-old lady with bunions in high heels gets you your drink by the time you're leaving. That's never the case at the Borgata.

I was playing and a waitress came up, and Melinda also walked up to me at the same time. I said to the waitress, "Hold on, you are distractingly attractive. I'd love another drink when you can." Melinda had heard me say shit like this before. She knew the game. She said to me, "Yeah, I'm leaving." I was like, "You have a key to the suite?" She said, "No, I'm leaving. I'm going home, packing my shit, and I'm moving out." I said, "Hold on!" and then to the dealer, "Hit me!" It was time to take a card. She thought it was going to be this dramatic conversation, and I just gave her nothing. I gave my hand that needed a card my attention and didn't even acknowledge her. I needed a seven and was doubling down. That was it—she turned and walked away. True to her word, she rented a U-Haul and took her stuff from my house before I even got back from my weekend in AC. A nine-year relationship ended at the high-rollers' table at the Borgata.

This was the beginning of a whole new world of fucking for me. I'd been married for nine years. The reason I got divorced was my girlfriend, Melinda, whom I was also with for nine years. I had been with only two girls (with the exception of the barmaid my wife had liked to sleep with) for eighteen years! This was during the time I was a radio star and making a shitload of money. It was my fucking prime, and I needed to make up for it in spades.

I decided I was going to fuck everything that would have me. That first weekend after the Borgata when Melinda left, I went to Opie's brother's restaurant, F. H. Riley's in Huntington, Long Island. There was some kind of O&A event going on there. Sometimes our amazing fans would pick a place and just get together. I would from time to time show up at these things, drinking and bullshitting with them, always having a fun time.

Well, this was my first time going to one of these events unattached and single. By the end of the night, I saw this overweight, disheveled chick who looked like she brushed her teeth with a rock. She was the only one left, and I bellied up to the bar and initiated a conversation with her. She started talking about my car and how she wanted to go for ride in my Mustang. Translation: she wanted to ride me! I was thinking, "Alright. This is it." I took her back to my house and we went at it. She was just a disaster. She stayed overnight. My friend Keith the cop came by the next morning, and I told her to hang upstairs and wait for me.

I didn't want anyone seeing my lapse of judgment with this atrocity that was lying naked in my bedroom. Keith just knew something was up. He fished, "Someone upstairs?" He started walking upstairs. "Hey, don't you fucking go up there!" I screamed. Keith was laughing his ass off because he totally knew what was up. It's almost a rite of passage that when you break up with someone after a long-term relationship, the next person you're with is never a prize. You don't want someone you'd risk falling for and wanting to be in another relationship with. The person is always a get-it-out-of-your-system girl. Keith found out who it was and just laughed at me. It was worth it because it broke my pattern of long-term relationships. I was now off and running.

Paltalk video conferencing was a gift from God to meet and hook up with women. It was international as well, and I was meeting women from all over. If I saw an attractive girl from, say, Ohio or Tennessee, I'd fly out there or fly them to New York. Within six months, I had been with ten times more girls than I had been with my entire life before that, and increased my frequent-flyer miles to boot.

Some of these women were cool, and some were mental patients. Some were pretty, and some were pigs. Keith the cop was beside himself. Aside from being my security specialist, he was a great friend. He didn't want to see "self-destructing Anthony," but at that point I was being pretty self-destructive.

One girl was from England, and she came to my house. I was fucking around with her and then I got an opportunity to go the Mohegan Sun casino in Connecticut with another girl. I left the chick from England at my house to go fuck another girl at a casino. Keith got wind that the girl from England was planning a party without my knowing or being there. He called and told me, "She's sending out messages for people to come to your house for a party, and I know you're not there." I was like, "Yeah, that can't happen." Keith said, "Alright, I got it." Keith went over there, sat her down, and had a talk with her. He said, "You're not having a party here, and you're going to have to go." He packed her suitcase, called her a cab, and sent her on her way. This was an example of what I was going through during what became years of just dating one girl after another. I wanted nothing to do with relationships anymore.

CHAPTER 18

The Howard Handshake

I WAS NOW A FREE spirit and could do as I pleased, which led me back to Atlantic City to do some more gambling at the Borgata. I went in one night, and as I was approaching the high-stakes tables, Howard Stern was already sitting down at a regular-stakes table playing cards with his crew, which included Artie Lange. My table wasn't directly next to his but was certainly in a nearby vicinity, where we could see each other. I don't know who saw whom first, but everyone on both of our sides was talking, like, "Hey, look who's here." I looked over and he saw me, and I said, "Hey, how ya doing?" He held up his stack of chips and said, "Eh, not too good." I motioned that I was just starting. Hoping for the best. It was very cordial. It was like the room sighed with relief. It felt like everyone had been waiting for something bad to happen and one of us to start in on the other. It was like in that movie *John Wick* when the assassins are at that one hotel where there's no killing allowed.

The Borgata was neutral sacred ground. If Opie had been there, it probably would have been a problem. Opie took the whole Howard thing way too personally, and he would have seen it as an opportunity to get some publicity. I did find it funny that Howard had a stack of white chips that were just worth one dollar apiece. His stack maybe equaled ten bucks. Meanwhile, I was walking in there with a stack of black hundred-dollar chips. He was playing the twenty-five- or fifty-cent table. I was a little surprised by his lack of cash at the table considering he'd just signed a half-billion-dollar deal with Sirius. He got up before I did and gave me a "have a good night" gesture, and that was it. In all those years, this was the only real interaction we ever had in person. I saw him only twice in the ten years I was in the Sirius building, and we worked the same hours.

The only time I ever shook Howard's hand was in the nineties, when I first started working with Opie on Long Island and did a Jackie Martling impression contest. I actually went on Howard's show as a contestant. I went with my buddy Randy, and Howard was like, "Who are you?" It was Christmastime and he was sitting there with a Santa hat on. I was just thrilled to be there. I had his *Crucified by the FCC* boxed set with me to be signed by him. I was ready to perform. If he gave me the opening, I was going to do everything I knew how to do. I knew it was the Jackie Martling contest, but I was doing everything! So I started by doing Jackie, and Howard was laughing. I then did Sam Kinison inviting Jackie to Vegas. There was a story going around about Sam asking Jackie to work with him in Vegas, and Jackie was harassing him about how much money he would be making. I started doing a back-and-forth of Jackie and Sam arguing over money. Howard was laughing his fucking balls off. He was like, "This guy is funny! He may look a little odd, but he's funny. I like Anthony, he's good." He asked, "What do you do?" I told him I was on the Opie show on Long Island. I got my plug in. I think Gary Dell'Abate, explained to him what the show was about. I was throwing everything against the wall hoping to get my foot in the door. I didn't win the contest, and I know it was because I mentioned Opie. If I hadn't mentioned I was working on the Opie show, I know I would have won. It was a thrill and really fun to do. I wanted to get my boxed set signed by Howard, and Gary said, "After the show." Then they just started shuffling everyone out and I never got the autograph.

CHAPTER 19

Sirius Days

THERE WAS ALWAYS A great group of characters who worked along with us. Our interns wound up doing really well. Sam Roberts was part of the first group of interns and is now doing the show with Jimmy. It's pretty amazing and cool to see that happen.

Opie always seemed to be heavy-handed with the staff, and I was the one who would be putting out the fires. I know Opie would say that he was the one putting out the fires that I started. The difference was that the fires I started were with management, which I considered a good thing.

If we were pissing management off, that meant the show was doing what it had to do. Opie was pissing people off like the producer, interns, and those who were working along with us on air. Those were the fires I was putting out. I'd always be like, "Well, that's just Opie. He's just really concerned about the show." Meanwhile, with every word coming out of my mouth, I felt like a battered wife. I had to explain the black eye. "I was just clumsy and fell into the doorknob. It's okay. Opie's a good guy." It was constant pressure. The only pressure I'd felt prior to XM was being more outrageous every day and satisfying the fans. The pressure I felt during XM was from trying to keep the whole thing together.

I was constantly working on keeping the problems Opie and I were having from affecting the show. Trying to keep staff problems from escalating, because that's when things could go sideways. Steve Carlesi, who was our producer for quite a few years, ended up getting fired. I don't think Opie liked him. We had conversations about Steve's shortcomings as a producer. He had a lot of positives too and was a really good guy.

You could get a hard-ass producer on a show who could mess everything up by being over-efficient. I always leaned toward producers who fit in. We weren't the most motivated motherfuckers either. It was nice to have someone who understood that and could work with us. About a year after Steve Carlesi was let go, he ended up killing himself. I don't think he ever got over the fact that he'd been fired. I never understood why he was let go. I never jumped in. I tried dealing with management as little as possible—especially at XM, because it was turning over so often. We wouldn't even know who owned the company sometimes.

It went from XM with one boss to having an interim CEO while a merger was being made. We knew this big merger wasn't going to favor us, with what we had going for ourselves. We had an amazing studio with great bosses who were giving us the flexibility to do what we wanted to do. When Sirius and XM merged, it was like saying, "When Nazi Germany and Poland merged." On March 28, 2008, the Justice Department officially approved the merger, and on November 18 the O&A channel would be carried on Sirius.

It was a sweeping takeover by Sirius of everything by XM. As I mentioned, XM had these eclectic visionaries who were doing something different from traditional radio. Those people from XM all got blown out and replaced by bean counters who did the top-twenty countdowns and other hack regular radio shit. A lot of the creativity went right out the door and, more important, so did support for our show. Sirius was Howard's company, and XM was our company. Now we were under the Sirius umbrella, and the *O&A* show could be like their 70s on 7 channel. They didn't give a shit about us, and we got nothing.

Once XM merged with Sirius, they were all about corporate, which translated to being censored for sexual content stringently. On April 14,

2009, we did our first show at the new Sirius building. There were no more girls doing the Wiffle ball bat contests or getting naked. In the bosses' eyes, these acts could make Sirius liable for litigation. This meant no more girls on our show unless it was a real interview. Sirius corporate was the ultimate cock blocker.

Meanwhile, Howard could have girls come on his show (literally) and get fucked on the Sybian machine while having bologna thrown on their tits. That's fair, right? This was the problem we had between Howard, management, and us. Taking away girls and sex was making our show very monotonous and mundane. We wanted to do fun, exciting things, and they just wouldn't let us. It was just like, "Go on the air and talk all day." That's what we did.

It became a talk interview show, which definitely wasn't the O&A show we were known for. It changed the complexion of the show. I think Opie appreciated that and preferred this new format, being that he was in a committed relationship. Jimmy and I were animals. We loved strippers, prostitutes, porno celebrities, and girls who wanted to do crazy shit. Opie was married and wanted to settle things down. He had in-laws now, who surely weren't thrilled about his being exposed to women getting naked and shoving things up their orifices.

In the early XM days, we did a thing called "Box of Cocks." It was a box with dildos glued to the bottom of it. We would put pictures of kittens on the outside and post a sign saying "free kittens" next to it, and leave it on 57th Street. We would hang out the window and watch inquisitive pedestrians who looked into the box expecting to see cute little kittens. The faces they made when they saw a plethora of dicks were priceless. Meanwhile, we weren't shooting video. It was us describing how each person was reacting.

All hilarious gags like this stopped. No more fun. No more sex. We were subjected to doing a show that anyone in any of the other glass studios could have been doing.

We moved from this amazing studio on 57th Street to a building on 48th Street that had no personality. We'd had the studio on 57th to ourselves, with no bosses in that building. It was great. Then they put us in a place with little hallways and identical cookie cutter studios. The studio we had was small, and when people wanted to come in, they had to have badges and be cleared by security. We used to have full bleachers of audience members at our 57th Street studio, which was filled really colorful characters we could work with. The new bosses took everything that was fun and different away from us. It was like stripping the powers from superheroes and asking them to still fight crime. This created enormous pressure. How could we get our audience members to tune in each day if we couldn't fucking do anything?

CHAPTER 20

In the Closet

I HAD A MAJOR CRUSH on the WPIX weekday traffic reporter, Jill Nicolini. Aside from working on Channel 11 news, she had been an actress and a model and had even posed naked in *Playboy*. She was absolutely beautiful and way the fuck out of my league.

Every morning she'd be up in the helicopter over the highways with a headset on, reporting the local traffic. We kept the TV on in the studio, and when Jill would be on camera, I would just look at her and say, "Oh my God, that girl is so hot." On our show, we'd talk about the other reporters on that station and their shit production value and would goof on them.

Jill eventually heard about my infatuation with her, and for my birthday she came into the studio with a birthday cake. I initially was having trouble forming words and was just babbling, in awe of her. She and I were talking superficially, and it wasn't that big a deal. I told her I thought she was pretty, and she was very sweet about it. She ended up coming in a few more times after that for other things. Anybody in any form of entertainment loves getting their name out there in another medium. We were a big show at the time and she liked being on, and we enjoyed having her.

She came on the show around May 2008, and I pulled the trigger and asked her out on a date while on the air, and she said yes. I was thinking, "She's doing this as a bit for the show. We'll go out to dinner, she'll say thanks, and that will be as far as it goes." I truly thought it would be something we could talk about on the show but that nothing would really come of it.

Having said that, I still was hoping in the back of my mind for the Hail Mary. I was gonna give it my best shot to impress this girl. My buddy Keith the cop worked in the Meatpacking District, which is where all the trendy restaurants were. I asked him, to hook me up with the best Italian restaurant he could find. He did and got me a great table with service that was impeccable. They just kept filling our wine glasses, and the food was amazing. They were treating us like we were their only patrons. I noticed there was something going on between Jill and me, and it was more than just a girl trying to get publicity. I thought she was liking this, and then I remembered feeling the same thing about a stripper at the Snatch Trap when I was kid with a handful of money. I knew it was the stripper's job, but I thought she liked me. Then I realized the reality after my money ran out and this broad started dry-humping my brother. So on this date with Jill, I was constantly on my guard, thinking she couldn't possibly be enjoying it as much as I was.

We finished dinner and were already a couple of bottles of wine in. We were buzzed and went to a bar to hang out—my ideal recipe for a great evening. We really started opening up and talking about everything. She actually had my same sense of humor, and we were clicking. I was making her laugh, and at some point it turned. We immediately went from this weird show *set-up* date to a *real date*. We started rubbing each other's hands and kissing.

Then we went back to her apartment in Long Island City, which is a hop, skip, and a jump from the bridge. Jill invited me in, and she had a beautiful place. We sat on her couch watching something on TV. I couldn't tell ya what, because I was completely preoccupied at this time. I'd made it this far. It felt like I was a soldier at Normandy: when I got off the landing craft, I immediately thought I was just gonna get shot in the head and it was gonna be over. I resigned myself to being dead. The further I worked myself up the beach, I gave myself a chance, thinking, "I just might make it! I just stumped a German machine gun nest, and I have one more move to take the bunker! I'm fucking right there!"

We were kissing on the couch and ended up in her bedroom. I think it was under the guise of, "We've been drinking, it's late, and we'll sleep it off here." My mindset was, "I'm going for that bunker." We started making out, and I was ready to get to business. She was like, "I don't know. This is all kind of quick." I was thinking, "Goddammit, I just saw one of those German hand grenades flying at me." I actually reverted into Anthony Cumia at the tender age of fifteen years old. This was one of those situations in which the best strategy is to take exactly what you did when a girl said the same thing when you were in high school.

I actually said, "Can I just put in the tip?" I swear, that's exactly what I said. I was a couple of years past my forty-fifth birthday when I asked her, "Can I just put in the tip?"

When I said this, she laughed her ass off. She thought it was the funniest thing, and let me put in the tip! At which point, much like in the video of the horse fucking the guy in the ass so hard it killed him, I pushed! The tip turned into balls-deep in two seconds. There's no "just the tip"! Everyone knows that! We both consensually realized this was happening, and we had a great night.

We woke up the next day and she looked at me and laughingly said, "Just the tip?" Meanwhile, I was in the apartment of the girl I've been gawking at on TV and just had sex with. We were lying in bed together and I realized you can never tell where anything is going in life. There was no way a week prior I could have possibly dreamed of this, but there I was.

I decided there was no way I was making it into work. I called into the show when they were live and said, "We're still on our date." Jill was laughing in the background. Opie actually got pissy with me that I took the day off. The whole buildup to it and the fact that I didn't come into work was because we spent the night together, and this was the best scenario for our listeners. It was fucking classic, and this was lost on Opie. I'd be in the next day and could talk about it then. All they were talking about was why I wasn't there. The fans were losing their minds. "He's not there, he's still with Jill Nicolini. He's banging the traffic girl! He did it!"

We spent that day taking her cat to the vet to get fixed. The cat was just giving her this look like, "Sure, you get laid all night and you're taking my ovaries out?" So, I was in the examining room with Jill, the cat, and the vet. The doctor was explaining how he was going to do the procedure and where he would be making the incision. Jill was completely engaged in the conversation, and I was fucking turning white, ready to faint. I can't watch shit like that and not get nauseous thinking about it. I was trying to be cool and excused myself with, "I'm going outside to smoke a cigarette." I hadn't smoked for years but had to get the hell out of there without blowing my cover for being such a pussy. I then went outside in front of the place with my head between my knees, trying to get blood back in my head. I felt a hand on my shoulder and it was her. "Okay, I was going to fucking faint. I'm such a faggot," I confessed.

We then went wine shopping. We did shit most couples do months into a relationship, even though we had been with each other only less than twenty-four hours.

The next day, I went back to the show and we were talking about my date. Jimmy said, "Do you love her?" I replied, "I think I love this girl." It was crazy, but I really felt something for her and was caught up in this whirlwind romance, which ended up lasting an entire summer.

Jill was pushing thirty and talking a lot about kids. I was constantly meeting members of her family—who were wonderful, by the way. As we were going through the summer, I started getting an inkling that she wanted a lot more than being just boyfriend and girlfriend.

I went out with her on a few of her appearances she made as a known TV personality. We once went to a country club for a charity event. She was walking around in this gown and was just stunning. Guys were drooling over her, and here was this lump-of-shit shock jock with his arm around her. I was the scourge of society. I had people fucking in church! We threw cherries and whipped cream in girls' assholes, and I was with the belle of the ball whom everyone wanted to ball. I was despised by everyone at every appearance I ever made with her. I was this piece of shit, and she was America's little sweetheart. I felt awkward and uncomfortable. Jill actually got a kick out of it and thought it was hilarious.

As time went by, I started thinking I didn't want to get "serious serious." I truly thought I loved her, which is so funny looking back now.

Then came the straw that broke the camel's back. A girl from Halifax, Canada, came down to New York. I had known her previously, and we'd had a fling a few years prior. This girl was really an incredible lay.

One time, I took this Halifax girl to the Atlantis hotel in the Bahamas and woke up and she was gone. She finally made her way back to our room, and I said, "What's up? Where were you?" She said, "I jumped the fence to swim with the dolphins, and I got high with them." She'd been smoking up and blowing her hits into the dolphins' blowholes while they were swimming up to her. I said, "Do you know how quick we'll get thrown out of here forever and sent to prison for getting dolphins high?" This broad was no Jane Goodall.

Then it was the end of August, and I always had a Labor Day pool party at my house. Jill wanted to take charge of the party planning. She was determined to make this into a Jill and Anthony party. She actually had cardboard cutouts of her and me with our arms around each other to put in the backyard.

The Canadian girl was cordially invited to the party. My instincts are not good when it comes to wanting to cheat. I'm the worst at it and always get busted. I wanted to hang out with the Canadian girl, and the two of us were in the Jacuzzi together. There were a lot of bubbles, with the opportunity to covertly do some touchy-feely underwater action. With the Canadian sitting next to me, I was sure that Jill's radar was tuned in to what was going on, and she was super suspicious. Jill gave me this look, and I knew she was pissed. I realized I could squash this problem by simply getting out of the Jacuzzi and rejoining the party, or I could just blow our whole relationship up and be with the Canadian girl. I decided on the latter.

Jill was fuming. She left the party and drove away in my Escalade. I didn't even care. I ended up in my bedroom with the Canadian getting some of that sweet poontang.

The Canadian girl and I were in bed, and I heard the Escalade pull into the driveway. I hadn't even thought of this scenario, and now there was no escape. I told the girl, "Get in the closet!" This naked girl from Halifax grabbed some clothes and ran for shelter. I have two big walk-in closets in the hallway that leads to the bathroom, and she went in the one to the left.

Jill now entered the house and made her way up to the bedroom. I was in bed and nervously said, "Hey, how ya doing?" I was shitting myself; it was just unbelievable. She came in for a kiss and then pulled the blankets back to start sucking my dick. She immediately pulled back and started moving her tongue up and down as if she were doing a taste test.

She suspiciously asked, "Hmm, what's that? That's someone else!" I quickly responded, "No it isn't. I don't know what you're talking about. Come on, this is crazy! This is insane!" She started looking around the room and headed right for the closets. She opened the door to the right, looked around, and then came back to the bed. I was thinking, "Oh my God, she didn't look in the left closet where the Canadian is hiding."

Now she really started giving me shit: "I saw you in the Jacuzzi, and you were all over the girl!" I went straight into denial mode: "No, no, no."

Then she got up and started heading to the other closet. I was just thinking, "Does the Canadian girl have a plan? Did she go between my clothes and at least make an attempt to hide?"

Jill opened the door, and the Canadian girl was sitting on the floor right in the middle of the closet with just a top on. She waved her hand and innocently whispered, "Hi." Like she was trying to do a Jedi mind trick. "This is not the Canadian you're looking for, and that taste in your mouth isn't from me."

Jill looked at me and stormed out of my house. I was relieved she was gone and that this was over. She took off in my Escalade, but before that she scooped up a bunch of shit, including the Canadian girl's backpack, my pistol license, and my wallet.

This was not good. The Canadian girl was freaking out. We left in my other car to get breakfast. While we were gone, Jill came back and went to the firepit in my backyard and burned everything she had taken. She set all the Canadian girl's stuff on fire. The Canadian girl had just smoked some weed and was mellow again, not letting much bother her. She was like, "Dude, I had taken my grandfather's ashes to be sprinkled in the Long Island Sound. That was in my backpack that she burned." I was like, "Well, it looks like your grandfather's final resting place is now the firepit in my backyard."

To this day, the Canadian girl's grandfather resides in the cracks and crevices of my firepit. There was a brassiere underwire smoldering in the ashes and all her clothes as well. I replaced everything and was able to once again have Keith come to the rescue. I had him go to Jill's and get back whatever she still had of mine that she hadn't already burned. That was the end of my swift romance with Jill Nicolini. It was zero to a hundred in three seconds. It was an amazing three months. I ran into her at some broadcasting function a few years later and she gave me some shit, but we ended up laughing, just as we had started.

The storied romance of "Antolini" played out like a marriage of fifty years in the span of three months.

CHAPTER 21

Is You Is or
Is You Ain't My Baby?

A**FTER I BROKE UP** with Melinda and Jill, I decided I wasn't going to be the typical boyfriend again. Of course, if you're gonna have sex with women, you have to put in some time—going out on dates, watching movies together—and they instantly deduce that you're their boyfriend. I didn't want to tell them this, because it would mess up any chance I had of getting laid. It was just so confusing. I think the last girl who was subjected to that kind of bullshit Anthony mentality was the model Melissa Stetten. She was a fan of the show and lived out in California.

Melissa messaged me on Facebook, and again with my great self-confidence I was thinking, "What kind of scam is this?" She was too good-looking. I thought, "This must be a really well-done catfish." I went through her social media and it had everything, with all kinds of pictures of her working as a model. One part of me was saying, "Maybe it's not someone catfishing me and it's legitimately Melissa." I was willing to make a complete asshole out of myself in order to have a shot at this.

I messaged her back and she gave me her phone number. It was the real deal. Here was this hot model and she wanted to hang out with me on a date. She was coming to NYC, and I was just flabbergasted.

I once again turned to Keith, asking him to get me a reservation at the best available restaurant in the city, and he did. We went to dinner, and a lot of the same things that had happened with Jill happened with Melissa. We instantly hit it off. I really dug this girl and she was stunningly beautiful. If memory serves me right, we had sex the first night in a hotel in Manhattan. We had a great time, and then came the continual phone calls asking, "What are you doing? Where do you want to go?" I was now feeling obligated and tied to this person. I needed to explain to her what I was doing, where I was, and when I was going to see her next. It was everything I didn't want. But it was too late, because now she was my *girlfriend*.

I did not stop looking for other girls. I was at Sirius XM and had Paltalk up. Every day I would look at the girls on the video feed and try to pick one. I'd start texting them my intentions and try to hook up. I would see that Melissa would also be on Paltalk. She'd be lying in bed with the camera on her, and she'd be looking at me. Now I was looking at her along with nine other girls on the screen whom I wanted to talk to and look at. Some of these chicks were naked and playing with themselves. I knew Melissa was looking at me, and if I wasn't looking directly at her, she would know that I was looking at other girls. It was quite the conundrum.

I tried looking at these other nude girls with a serious face, like I was typing. It was as if I weren't even looking at Paltalk, as if I were doing some serious work with my serious face. I was watching this girl fingering herself in bed while I was pretending to be improving my typing speed. I didn't want Melissa to know.

I was never monogamous with her. I was constantly on the hunt for vagina, and I found it. Melissa was always suspicious.

One time we were at the Parker Meridien hotel ready to go out for a night in the city. I went to take a shower, and it didn't even occur to me that I had left my cellphone in the room. I also don't turn off the beginnings of text messages. When I receive a text, it makes a buzzing noise, then displays the beginning of that text. It shows who it's from and a sentence or two. This time I got a text from a girl, and it was something like, "I can't wait until we can…" The rest of that sentence certainly wasn't "discuss your stock options with our hedge fund." It obviously was "until we can have some sex."

I was in the shower innocently partaking in my evening ablutions when Melissa started screaming, "You motherfucker!" I couldn't quite hear what she was saying. I then opened the door and actually said, "What, baby?" I then clearly heard her say, "You motherfucker!" All of a sudden, the phone came flying in, hitting me directly on the side of my head. The phone made its way to the bottom of the shower by the drain. It was now a soaking-wet dead iPhone. My head hurt and I was being yelled at by my girlfriend who really wasn't my girlfriend. I did the first thing every guy does and pleaded innocent: "What? I don't even know what you're talking about." Meanwhile, I knew exactly what the fuck she was talking about. You don't have to be Columbo to put the evidence together. Girl throws phone at your head and says, "Fuck you!" Hmm, I wonder. That ruined that night.

We kind of brought things back together after that, but she never trusted me again. She knew I was constantly carousing, and she was too. When she'd take trips back home to California, God knows what she was doing there. I didn't give a shit. At that point, I didn't care about our relationship. I was like, "If you're around, we'll hang out; if not, whatever. I don't want to hear stories about mega-dong black cock in you while you're in California. That said, I don't really care what you do."

That wasn't good for her. She moved back to California and hooked up with James Gunn, who was the writer, producer, and director of the blockbuster hit movie *Guardians of the Galaxy*. He also had written the film *Dawn of the Dead*, which I thought was hilarious. When I heard she was now dating James Gunn, I was like, "Oh fuck, he's a lot more successful than I am." This was well before *Guardians of the Galaxy*, which put him way over the top. He moved Melissa and himself to London, England, to write the movie. She was putting shit up on Facebook and Instagram like, "This is the dog that inspired him for the character Rocket." Right before he was ready to submit the last version of the screenplay and start filming, he told her to take a plane back to LA. The guy ended up being one of the most successful Marvel writers ever, and there was poor Melissa once again shoved back to LA to model at thirty-plus years of age. I really wish her the best. Every once in a while, on a cold day, I can still see the imprint of the iPhone on the side of my head.

After Melissa, I made a concerted effort to start telling girls right away that we were not going to be boyfriend and girlfriend. We could hang out and have a great time without any obligation to each other.

In the beginning it was, "Of course. Thank God you said that! That's exactly what I want!" I'd always reply, "This is awesome. Good. Glad we understand each other."

Then because I was nice and did the dinners along with the fun cool nights of just hanging out making jokes, next thing I knew, we were a fucking couple.

"What happened? I thought you were cool just keeping this casual."

They'd start crying, "I have feelings for you. It just happened."

Then we'd end up becoming boyfriend and girlfriend because nothing else works and this system is insane. I still can't figure it out.

CHAPTER 22

Ding Ding: In This Corner

O<small>N</small> M<small>ARCH</small> 12, 2009, Opie and I had an on-air fight known as "the Grape Argument." I was eating grapes on the air. I remarked on something, and Opie said, "Are you gonna wait till you finish those?" This argument had nothing to do with the fucking grapes. It was like any argument: you start out with the issue and then it just splinters into a thousand things that pissed you off ten years prior. He was obviously mad at something.

So, I said, "Oh really? You're gonna give me shit about the grapes? I could read you twenty texts about you scraping your yogurt container!" How petty was this? He gave me this face that I knew all too well. This pissed-off face. Opie kept saying, "Leave it alone," but I didn't want to leave it alone. Then he quipped, "Just because you're really into doing the show again, leave it alone!" to which I replied, "As opposed to when I really wasn't into doing the show?" That was it! I saw fucking red. He had passive-aggressively suggested I wasn't into the show for a certain period of time. Opie then said, "Don't worry, dude. This will be over soon. You go your way and I'll go mine."

How prophetic he was. For months he had been alluding to this inevitable breakup on air. "It's just time for us to break up. We've done everything there is to do together, and it's time for us to move on to some new challenges." I told him, "I actually enjoy coming in here to do this show and don't bitch about every little thing going on. I try and keep it light."

Opie just started giving me a litany of gripes he had against me. He complained I was constantly on my phone and missing a lot of shows due to whatever the fuck I had going on in my life. Then I called him out on his bullshit. The personal days he had taken off and the time he had questioned my sick day when I legitimately had a fever and the flu.

One of his biggest points of the argument was that I had called out with little to no notice. He then said he "could do other things." I fired back, "No you couldn't!" and he replied, "I could easily do another show!" I told him, "What are you gonna do, spin records again?" He said, "What are you gonna do, make fun of me? My whole problem with you isn't that I don't like you or respect you. I just think we're moving in two different directions. We've made a great living together for fourteen years, and I'd rather move on before things get ugly."

We both knew there were feelings of resentment and animosity that had been percolating for a long time. Opie made it very clear he wanted to split up. He basically was proposing a split right then and there. The irony is that even when we were fighting, we did great radio together. That segment was entertaining, compelling, and, yes, still funny. Toward the very end of this segment, things were starting to cool down, and I said, "Hey, do you want a grape?" Classic.

One year into our run at WNEW, we brought Jim Norton on to the show as a regular. He originally came on as a guest with Andrew "Dice" Clay and was clearly something very special. He stuck out and was just killing it. We eventually started having him come on by himself, and he was consistently funny and said and thought about things Opie and I didn't. A lot of funny people came on, but Jimmy fit on the show perfectly.

He started joining us two or three times a week. His becoming a full-time member was a slow, natural evolution. Then we got him some money to come in. The station started paying him, and it was working very nicely. Opie went balls-out to get Jimmy on the show. With the "Melinda situation," I think Jimmy might have seen we were not as friendly as we'd used to be and that we should get someone else in there to be a buffer.

One day I walked into work very close to six again, and Opie was pissed. I sat down in my seat, and I was watching him talk to Jimmy. He purposely went out of his way not to make eye contact with me.

That was his tactic of letting me know he was mad—not looking at me. I grabbed my phone and texted Jimmy saying, "The fucking cunt won't even make eye contact with me!" and I hit send and it went to Opie! I had accidentally sent it to Opie! I put the phone down and just sat and stared at Opie's phone, and I saw it light up with the text I'd sent.

I saw him look at his phone. Then he looked at me and said, "What the fuck is this?!" I was like, "What?" "This!" he said, holding up his phone. "Oh, yeah I was talking about, um…" I was trying to lie, and then I realized there wasn't any getting out of it and just said, "Yeah, well, you're fucking not, so fuck you!" This was two minutes before showtime. He was like, "You motherfucker! Fuck you! Who were you sending this to?" I quickly responded, "My chick!" I didn't want to hang Jimmy out to dry. So I told him I was sending it to my girlfriend at the time, Melissa. He got livid and left the studio. He left the show.

The other time he refused to work with me was when I went to his brother's restaurant and couldn't get a beer. No one was serving me, so I did what any grown man would do: I tweeted. I wrote, "Geez you would think I could get a fucking beer here!" Opie got so pissed and lost his mind. He was wondering why I hadn't just texted him. He was being protective of his brother's place, which I totally get.

I was already annoyed at him overall and thought it was a good way to piss him off. Immature? Yeah. Enjoyable? Absolutely. He didn't come to work for two days. I showed up two days in a row and did the show with Jimmy. It was great, but my boss told me, "You'd better fucking apologize to him!" Opie wasn't showing up to work, and I was the one who had to square it. They knew he wasn't coming in till I apologized. Everyone knew Opie was the sensitive one. I bit my tongue and said, "I'm sorry," and he eventually came back.

I apologized for the text and the tweet. I constantly felt like I was with a chick. It was like having a girlfriend. You have words with a guy buddy and it usually goes, "I was being an asshole." "It's okay, bro, go fuck yourself!" "Okay, man, let's have a beer." "Okay cool."

With Opie it was like, "Ya know, when we communicate I really feel like you're not opening up enough." What the fuck? What was this? Guys don't talk this way. We'd been running like this for a while. The shows were great, but we knew there was a dark cloud over the studio. That said, we didn't let it affect the show.

It was always an issue when Opie was in a room or studio with a bunch of comics. Patrice O'Neal, Rich Vos, Jimmy Norton, and Colin Quinn. We would be trading barbs and just laughing our asses off. Nothing funnier than being in the barrel. You say something stupid, they all fuckin' jump on you. You're in it. You're trying to battle to get out. I love that shit. It's like a game. Opie would sit there like the kid who didn't want to be called on by the teacher. Like, "Don't mention my name, don't point at me." I think his not being a part of that brought on a lot of animosity.

We were all laughing and having a great time, and he was the one who had to say, "Okay, let's take a break." The listeners were like, "Really, man? You're gonna stop these guys?" He had a job to logistically structure the show, but to the listener, everyone was having fun and he was the guy who just cut it off. So, he caught shit for it, and I think he didn't have the personality and thick skin to handle it. He would take a lot of that shit personally. The comics were aware of this. I'd see some of the most vicious comics not saying anything to him, and I'd know why they weren't doing it. Everyone in the room was supposedly fair game, and we'd get some of the funniest guys who could rip anyone apart not giving him one bit of flack, because they knew he might just not invite them back.

That was the dynamic between the comics and Opie at that point. Opie would give Rich Vos shit. Rich was an easy target for everyone. "Oh, you're stupid and you can't spell and you talk funny." Rich is known for destroying and picking apart his audiences unmercifully, and yet he always gave Opie a pass. It didn't build any animosity with me or the comics, because there were plenty of people to rag on in the room. It built up Opie's animosity because he knew he couldn't hang in the barrel. He knew he wasn't up to snuff, and it made him feel inadequate.

After a while, the resentment started to rear its ugly head, because I think he saw his role becoming diminished in the actual stuff that was going out over the air. You want to hear, "Holy fuck, that was hilarious! Wow, that was funny! You and Rich today! You and Jimmy!" It was always Jimmy and me connecting comedically with our guests or each other. Jimmy and I had this sixth-sense chemistry that was at a whole different level. Opie started getting like, "Huh, I'm pretty utilitarian here." Even though he was the one driving this funny fuckin' show in the right direction. That isn't what people comment on social media about. You never heard people giving him the accolades, like, "You really know how to navigate the funny guys."

To say the popularity of our show went to Opie's head would be an understatement. He had this delusion that we were so big, we needed security to protect us. I understood if we were out at a bar doing a show and there was the possibly that someone drunk could get rambunctious. But it actually got to the point at Sirius where "Club Soda" Kenny would walk Opie from our studio to the bathroom in our already overly secure high-rise building.

What the fuck could possibly happen in between the studio and the bathroom? It's a hallway in an office space that's run by Sirius. It was this weird elevated sense of importance that Opie constantly had. He figured if he needed security to walk him to the bathroom, he must be a big shot. The reality was, he *told* the security guard to walk him to the bathroom. I would get up to go to the bathroom sometimes, and Kenny would get ready to walk me and I'd say, "Kenny, I think I'm okay. I can make it to the bathroom and hold my own dick while I pee."

Kenny would walk Opie everywhere, from the parking garage to places he went outside the building after the show. He would drive him home after the show. It made no sense whatsoever that either of us would need a security guard. Howard Stern was a different story, and I think that always tortured Opie.

Howard had something, and Opie wanted the same thing because he thought he was just as big, good, and important as Howard. I was like, "No, Howard really does need security. He has fans everywhere that want to mob the guy. He's one of the most recognizable stars in the world."

We would walk outside and occasionally there'd be two or three people who'd want to take a picture, which was fine. If Howard had walked out every day, there would have been a crowd of people wanting his picture, and someone could possibly have gotten out of hand. He'd have needed a guy there so he could get to his car safely.

Opie had that in his head and wanted the same shit Howard had. He couldn't understand why we weren't getting it from the company. It was absurd to try to compare our celebrity status with Howard's. Every time Opie would leave to go to the bathroom with Kenny escorting him, the second the door would close we'd break out in laughter. What the fuck? Was the 70s on 7 girl DJ going to take a poke at him? Was Martha Quinn from MTV going to smack him or something? Fame went to his head more than anyone else's. I always took everything with a grain of salt and with the idea that I couldn't even believe any of this was happening.

We'd go to a club and there were a lot of fans while we'd do our stage show. Opie would want a VIP area backstage and to be ushered out to a waiting vehicle. I would finish and head for the bar to hang out with people and drink. I'd be doing shots and enjoying myself. Opie thought if he did this, he would be mobbed and surrounded by people bugging him for autographs. I think that he knew deep down inside it wouldn't happen, and didn't want to fuck up his fantasy.

If he had gone to the bar and didn't have a bunch of people clamoring around him, his fantasy of being more than what he really was would instantly have been shattered. I loved the interaction with our fans and always had a blast. It was like a built-in party that I was the host of but didn't have to worry about cleaning up after. Fans would constantly call Opie out on that.

Opie blew me off and didn't talk to me. We definitely had a different way of approaching our fans and dealing with them. I always felt like it was a mutual one-on-one, *mano a mano* thing. His idea was pure fantasy. He lived his life like that fantasy was the reality. He sequestered himself. He wouldn't let people see pictures of him or his family. Really? What was he, John Paul Getty? If he didn't want to put pictures out there, that was fine, but I know why he didn't. It was to perpetuate this false fantasy that there were droves of people wishing to do him some type of harm—more than just websites calling him an asshole. It was never the case.

I will say, I appreciated and understood the importance of his role. But for Opie, the guy who started the show, to not receive praise…well, it started getting to him. I think of that movie *The Prestige*, in which Hugh Jackman has to drop under the stage and his look-alike comes up and takes the bows for the biggest trick he did. He's under the stage listening to the crowd explode and loving it. But he's like, "Fuck, I'm not the one standing in front of the audience." That's exactly what I think Opie started feeling at some point—almost ignored and taken for granted. It was one of those behind-the-scenes things.

Because of this, he would act out and take it out on other people, one of whom was yours truly.

I'm not trying to make myself out to be golden. Truth is, I brought many negatives to the table too, but I always felt that the fans of the show gravitated toward me because I made myself available to them. I'd tweet, "I'm gonna be jamming with my brother at this bar. Come on out." Or, "I'm gonna be partying [wherever] tonight!" Opie was much more private, and I certainly didn't fault him for that. But the fans knew I was more accessible, and it resonated with them and I feel it made me more popular in their eyes. They would say, "I was with Anthony last night. Holy shit, I had a blast! Really cool, hung out and talked for a while." Opie was standoffish to most fans.

When social media really started kicking up, it became obvious there was a fucking hatred of Opie. It was so weird, because it was almost too much. It was like this guy had to have done something to the show's fans personally for them to have said this kind of vicious shit about him. It turned out they just didn't like him. I had my share of that as well. People said terrible things, but it's part of the game. I like snipping back at them and dishing it out too.

CHAPTER 23

The Tweet Heard
Round the World

I HAD JUST FINISHED DOING the TV show *Red Eye* on Fox News, and I went over to a great karaoke bar, Tonic, to sing a few tunes. It was around 3:30 a.m. and I decided that since I had this great camera on me, as well as a few drinks in my system, it would be a good idea to take some pictures of Times Square. The most photographed place on earth, right? It wasn't this odd thing, like, "What's this guy doing taking pictures at this time of night?"

It's actually the perfect time to snap a few clicks there, because there aren't many people around and it's still all lit up and perfect to shoot. On this night, there was scaffolding on the sidewalk, and the bare light bulbs hanging down made this great tunnel effect going toward where they drop the ball for New Year's Eve. I thought it made for a great shot.

I started snapping, and the camera was loud. It was a Canon reflex that made this *chi-ching, chi-ching* sound. There was a girl on the sidewalk walking away from me, and she heard the camera and all of a sudden turned around and said, "Uh-uh!" Then she was running toward me like a lion after an antelope, calling me a white motherfucker, and started smacking me in the fucking face. I was taking shots to my head. They were open-hand smacks. She was screaming, "You don't take pictures of me!" I told her, "I wasn't taking pictures of you!" There was no talking to her; she was in a rage. But I never felt that she was even close to threatening my life, and she wasn't hurting me.

I was pissed but wasn't going to do anything. Certainly not retaliate physically. Then a couple of guys came over and said, "Don't you put your hands on her!" I said, "I'm not touching her!" I was putting my hand up to stop her from hitting me, and I had the other one down to protect my camera and my balls.

I totally de-escalated the situation and went back to my apartment, which was two blocks away. I got there and was fuming—full of piss and vinegar. I was really angry, so I decided to do what any grown man in my position would do: I tweeted.

If I made any mistake, it was tweeting some social commentary along with a detailed description of what I had just gone through. If I had just documented what had happened, it might have been one thing, but I wrote some stuff like, "This woman was an animal!" and "Savage behavior!" I never said anything racist about it, however.

It's amazing how social media misinterpreted my account of the assault on me and my anger toward this despicable person as being racist. For the record, I am not and have never been racist. I judge people as individuals. I know the reputation I've gotten over the years, and I play that as a character. I make jokes about it. If someone brings up a racial issue, I push it to the furthest I can take it, but it's funny. It's a joke. I'm playing off the reputation I've gotten off people who really don't even know me from a hole in the wall. Truthfully, it does bother me that I'm falsely associated with this stigma, because things like this on the internet live forever and there's no knocking them down. I got railroaded, big time.

The media called it a "racial tirade." I've said a lot worse things on the airwaves at Sirius than anything I've ever tweeted, and there were never any ramifications. But off the air, I got assaulted and voiced my displeasure and got fired. Sirius used my tweets as an excuse to fire me. I think they just wanted to free up some money in the budget. I was making a lot of money, and they thought they could get rid of me and probably still hold on to listeners by holding on to Opie and Jimmy.

In the past, Opie and I had always been fired together, and I'd never worried about it as long as our ratings were up and we had a strong fan base. This was the first time I was solo. I was like, "Oh fuck! Now what?" Initially I thought I could move to Pennsylvania and get a house. I had this whole scenario of uprooting everything. Why would I stay in Long Island without a job? I was gonna pay a mortgage on a house in Roslyn Heights? I started to reassess everything I was doing.

The first day after I was fired, I had my infamous Fourth of July party. I had at least eighty people at my house partying with me; meanwhile, I had no idea what my fucking life was becoming. I had no idea what I was doing. Finally, when the music stopped and all the drinks were drunk, people started filing out of my house, and that's when it really settled in: "What the fuck am I gonna do now? I'm stuck! I'm damaged goods!" Luckily, when I was fired, I still had a huge loyal fan base that wanted me to keep doing what I loved, which was being on the radio. And it was because of the fans' support that I knew I wanted to keep doing this.

Since the firing until this very day, I have not spoken to Opie privately. We've texted and spoken via my podcast, but he never reached out to me when I got fired. I expected a little more from him. The thing that really got me is when they went live for the first time after I got fired. First of all, I was hoping they'd hold off on the show and say, "Hey, let's try and get Anthony back." Something. Just some kind of indication that Opie gave a fuck that I'd been fired after we'd been doing a show together for almost twenty years. That showed me a boatload about not only the way he felt about me but also how he felt about the show.

He apparently didn't enjoy what we had been doing. If he truly did, he would have tried to keep me on. I think Opie felt like he could do a show without me or Jimmy, and if it was successful, it would justify his talent. He'd be like, "See, I didn't need him after all." Again, as a human being, I'm glad that didn't happen. It validated me and what I knew I had brought to the show all those years. I would have hated it if things had gone well and it had been business as usual.

Fortunately, that wasn't the case.

Once I was fired, it was *The Opie Show with Jim Norton.* Jimmy didn't want his name on that show. He specifically wanted it to be "with Jim Norton" as opposed to *The Opie and Jim Show,* because he knew it was going to be a disaster in the making. They just did not get along. I knew without me as a buffer, they would not last a year with each other, and I was right. They were just like oil and water. Jimmy could not get out of there fast enough. They had zero chemistry and couldn't make it work. I knew I was that common denominator for those two to work well with each other. I knew and understood Jimmy, and I knew and understood Opie, and I could work as the go-between.

I listened to the beginning of that first show, and I was pissed. I was pissed at that bitch in Times Square for slapping me in the head, I was pissed at Sirius XM, and I was pissed at the people on the show. Overall, I was pissed I was sitting home with no prospects. No one was calling me with job opportunities. My agent wasn't telling me about a ton of offers pouring in. So, I was just fucking angry, depressed, and uncertain where I was going. Opie and Jimmy started talking about my getting fired right away, and it was surreal to hear them talking about me and I wasn't there. Opie was saying it was "so weird, man." Honestly, I didn't really feel any sincerity there about how weird it was. He never put across on that show that he was unhappy that it had happened. I know he wanted me gone. I never got from Opie that he was upset about my firing. It seemed like he was ready to move on, and at that point, truthfully, so was I.

Opie and I had a personal relationship for twenty years that went beyond our professional one. It started out that we were very good friends. We did a lot of hanging together outside of work, and like at work, we seemed to complement each other socially. It's ironic that our show flourished regardless of our faltering friendship. I think our friendship and the show were so intertwined early on that one really depended on the other. It was so important for us to be very close.

Toward the end, Opie and I were cognizant of the fact that the only thing we had together was the show. That was it. Which I was fine with. I've been in friendships that have gotten better over the years and some that have gotten worse. I have friends I've had since 1977 in high school, and we're still as tight as we were back then. Every party we're at, we love each other. I have other people I thought would be my best friends forever, and within a couple of years, with either moving or a new job, I never heard from them again. I just chalk that up to what we were. Opie and I had this show in common.

There was no Opie without Anthony, and conversely, there certainly wasn't an Anthony without Opie. I could never have walked into a radio studio as a high school dropout construction worker and say, "Hey, where's my mic? Where do I go here?"

We both did each other justice. The sum of the two of us made one of the most amazing radio shows that ever was. We owe each other immensely for what we both did together, which we couldn't have done individually.

The *Opie and Anthony* show was a wild ride that ended in 2014. Little did I know a new ride was just beginning.

CHAPTER 24

The Birth of Compound Media

I'M OFTEN ASKED ABOUT Keith Maresca, aka Keith the cop. How'd we first meet? What's his role in my life and in Compound Media?

Well, here it is:

Back in the *O&A* days, we had an intern named Spaz who needed a police uniform for a bit we were doing. Some girl wanted to have her birthday party in the studio, and we were doing a Village People theme with the Indian, construction worker, and cop. We got on the radio and said, "Is there anybody who can bring us a police uniform for this intern?" Keith Maresca had been listening and was a fan of the show. He had never called in or had any interaction with us prior to that. He then called in and said, "I have a uniform."

Opie answered the phone, and Keith drove over and dropped off the uniform. The bit worked out, and we took down his information. He worked for the NYPD and said if we ever needed a cop for a bit, we could call him. He was a cool guy who understood what we were doing on the show and loved listening in his patrol car. Keith was a cop who became a sergeant, then a lieutenant, and later retired in 2012.

In December 1999 we started doing a homeless shopping spree. We took a bunch of homeless people to the very upscale shopping center The Mall at Short Hills, located in Short Hills, New Jersey. We got them all tanked up on beer on the bus. Then we unleashed these drunk homeless people on one of the most high-end shopping malls in the country. We gave them each a hundred dollars. The stores started frantically pulling down their gates, not wanting them to shop there. We had hundreds or possibly a thousand fans come out yelling, "Let them shop! Let them shop! Let them shop! Let them shop!" The stores had to lift the gates and let them in. These fans also gave the homeless people money on top of what we had given them to shop. *O&A* fans rock! The fans made sure they all had boots and warm coats for the winter. These homeless people weren't the crazy types who would hurt someone. They were mostly really cool people who were either alcoholics or down on their luck.

Keith was the one who had gotten us the homeless people from around his precinct, and he really enjoyed giving them this great experience before the holidays. Keith actually went on the bus with them to make sure everything was done within the correct boundaries. Sometimes even our show's craziness paid off in a benevolent way.

After the homeless shopping spree, Keith the cop became a friend of the show, and we started using him and "Club Soda" Kenny for security at events with a lot of people in attendance. "Club Soda" Kenny was with Opie, and Keith was with me.

When we went to XM, Master Po was our security guy. I have no idea how this guy got the gig. He fancied himself a karate expert. He was this tall Puerto Rican with long hair and a goatee. There were videos of him with bamboo sticks, knives, and swords. We were always like, "This guy is so ridiculous." He went with us as security on the walk from K-Rock to our XM studio, because we never knew what could happen. One time a guy started yelling something to Opie about Howard Stern, and Master Po just jumped on this guy, putting him in a chokehold. Master Po wasn't fucking around. This guy really wanted to earn his keep. Management did not like that and suggested that we obtain a professional security guy.

We then hired Keith to do security for us, and his wife, Angela, became and is still my personal assistant. Angela had been laid off from her job at Bloomingdale's, and I had recently purchased my home in Roslyn. It was sparsely decorated, and Ange said, "If you'd like me to decorate your home for you, let me know." It's a big home. It's the type of house that requires a professional to come in with some interior design knowledge, which she had. I told her, "Please!" At that point, I had already been there with Melinda for a year, and people would come over and be like, "Did you just move in?" All I had was a folding card table (with my computer on it to play video games), a plasma television, and a Mets bean bag chair that I would drink red wine while watching TV in. The entire rest of the house was empty. Ange decorated the whole house, and when she was done I hired her to take care of all the incidentals, including my home and everything else. I don't think I could function without her. Keith and Ange are family to me. We share everything from holidays to vacations with one another.

Keith is someone who has my best interest in mind always. I don't take that lightly.

☙

Since July 2014, when I was fired, up to this very day, the idea of working for a company has only gotten more nightmarish. Especially with the type of content I do. If I hadn't been fired for the tweets, I'd have been fired five more times in between then and now for something else. I honestly know I would have done or said something that would have forced them to get rid of me. It's just gotten significantly worse with the need to be politically correct.

The persecution of people who are speaking openly and honestly is insane. Comedy has been becoming something that's hate speech in certain people's eyes and to their ears. This situation, coupled with my having built a constant momentum since 2014, was perfect timing with a Trump presidency. It's all coming together and has absolutely been a blessing in disguise. Currently there's nothing more relevant or in demand than a podcast. It's now the thing to do. Broadcast companies don't want personality-driven programming. They say they do sometimes, but for the most part, regular FM radio wants monkeys spinning records and shutting their mouths. Satellite radio wants irreverent speech within some very narrow margins. It's not the unbelievable place where free speech resides anymore. Sirius is a company with board members and advertisers—and all those can be attacked when a group says a jock did something offensive. If you want honest, actual, true freedom of speech, it has to be just you. It has to be that you're the guy and you have to talk about anything and everything—good, bad, or indifferent.

When I was fired from Sirius, I was damaged goods and exiled from show business for my crimes on Twitter. I was actually thinking, "I'll move to Pennsylvania and start a militia." Keith came over to the house and said, "You know, you have that studio in the basement; why don't you do a show from here?" As far as motivation goes, I normally have none. I really do need that kick in the ass to get things going. Keith the cop was that kick in the ass.

All I was thinking about were the negatives. How the fuck would I even do it? I would pop on at 2:00 a.m. on a Friday drunk off my ass. I'd tweet I was doing a show and get a couple of hundred people on, whatever. I'd have some fun and shut it down.

How do you put a show out for thousands and thousands of people? How do you monetize it? You have to figure out the logistics of how to actually get it from the studio to a medium where people know where it is. I just couldn't imagine how to even start.

Keith said, "We'll just take it one step at a time. We'll call this guy about servers and another guy about creating a website. We'll just figure it out." Alright, sounded good. I would handle the creative end, and he would concentrate on the logistics. I give all the credit to Keith. He's the kind of guy who can yell like no one else on a phone to make things happen and get shit done. I'm not that guy.

I was deciding on what type of show I was going to do. Was it going to be comedy or political? Was it going to be just me? How did I want it presented to people? It was a total work in progress.

As far as I know, I was the first person to do a live-streaming podcast. Most people taped their podcasts and then put them out. Also, most podcasts prior to mine weren't visual. We are in such a visual world now that audio alone just doesn't cut it. Toward the end of my run on Sirius, we were discussing videos and trying to describe them on the air. I wanted to do a show on which my audience could see and hear me live. Now that's walking on a tightrope without a fucking net.

We decided to take a month to get everything set up, and then we'd go live. I chose 4:00 to 6:00 p.m. Monday through Thursday. Why? I could be up by four, and if I was done by six, I could still go out. Why four days a week? Three-day weekends are awesome. I had no rhyme or reason in selecting these times or schedule. It wasn't like we did surveys and learned that most people listen to podcasts between this time and that time. Nah, I just didn't want to get up early anymore.

Finally, I was the boss and could make my own rules. I wanted to give the audience an option to catch the show live or watch it on demand afterward. It worked well. The time, duration, and number of days were right on the money and are still what I'm working with.

It was so stressful trying to get this new live-streaming podcast up to speed and making it the show I wanted to do. It was nerve-racking, and I don't like being nervous on the air. I don't like being in a position where I'm not at my best. This was such a new medium for me that I never felt comfortable for that first year. I felt like I was forcing it.

This was all riding on me. I didn't have anyone else to lean on. If they had put me on the mic at Sirius alone, I would have done the show. There were times Opie was out and it was just Jimmy and me running the show. This was never a problem, and Opie always came back.

This new subscription podcast was all on my back. If it failed, it would be my failure.

Once we had everything in place and announced what we were doing, we launched the website and started taking subscriptions. It was like Obamacare, and the site crashed. I was just beside myself thinking, "Right out of the box! I'm a failure before I'm even on the air." On the one hand, it was great that so many people wanted to sign up, but in my head I was like, "If people can't subscribe today, they're not gonna try again. It's never gonna work."

We got the site back up and started getting subscription orders before we even went live. Now it was really the time for me to go, "Now what?"

I had never done a show by myself aside from *Live at the Compound*, when it was whoever wanted to tune in and we weren't collecting money for a real show. I hadn't been obligated to give anyone anything. Now I was taking a subscription fee, and my being drunk at 3:00 a.m. wasn't going to cut it. I needed to be consistent and come up with some type of real structure. It was an on-the-job learning experience, and we hoped if we didn't fuck up that bad, we wouldn't chase any of our subscribers away. We would just go on every day and cross our fingers that the equipment worked and that I was able to put on a couple of hours of entertainment that was received well enough for people to come back the next day.

I wasn't doing my show from Manhattan anymore either. I was doing it out of my home in Roslyn Heights, which was a forty-five-minute drive from the city without traffic. It wasn't going to be a picnic getting guests to make that trek out there. Most of my guests wanted to promote stuff and were already doing the circuit of talk shows in NYC, where they could knock them all out at once. Coming to Roslyn wasn't ideal.

I had my comic friends, the ones who hadn't pulled the plug on me, come out and do the show. There were some comics who didn't like what I'd been fired for, who'd heard only one side of the story—the online side that had painted me falsely as a racist. Comics who'd once been happy as fuck to get on the *O&A* show backed off, distancing themselves from me.

Jim Breuer dropped off the face of the earth. I never heard from him again. I'm certain it had to do with the shit he read online about me. I was thinking, "Talk to me about it and get my take on things before ostracizing me."

There was a good year or so with no communication between Joe Derosa and me. He thought, "How am I supposed to explain to my black friends that I'm friends with Anthony Cumia?" After a year we got on the phone and talked about it. Literally within three minutes, we were laughing our asses off and calling each other an idiot. Even that was weird, because looking back, I'm like, "Why the fuck didn't you call me and ask what happened, instead of reading something on Buzzfeed or something? All of a sudden, I'm a fucking asshole? You should know all that shit was completely blown out of proportion and distorted."

Bill Burr also took issue with me when this happened. After all the years of sitting there with me talking about shit on the show, understanding what I was saying, what was a joke and what was serious, I thought he'd have a little more insight into who I was as a real person—that he wouldn't have just thought I was the piece of shit they were portraying in these online articles. Bill and I later "smoked the peace pipe "during one of Patrice O'Neal's benefit shows and hashed everything out. We're cool now.

There are comics I like and currently talk to who I think still have a problem with me and won't come on my show. I'm not going to out who they are, because I still have contact with them. I know they're a little shy and shaky about doing my show. They're thinking, "What would my friends say? What would Comedy Central executives say?" Everyone is just trying to get that next gig. I understand that, but at what cost?

Guests weren't the biggest thing for this project. More times than not, especially on the *O&A* show, I had looked at guests as a speed bump and a detriment to what I wanted to do with Jim Norton on that show:

talk about the news and what was going on in our lives and make it hilarious. We'd be right in the middle of it and would be interrupted with, "Oh, we have the guitarist from some band or a wrestler guy who just came in." I'd be like, "Fuck!" It was such a niche fan who wanted to hear about that guest, and it would just derail everything.

The Anthony Cumia Show was mostly just focused on me, along with the visual aspect of my playing clips from YouTube and the news. It wasn't going to be a clip show, like MTV's *Virtual Hills*. The visual stuff would supplement what I was discussing more than my just discussing what was on the screen. Having guests coming out to Roslyn wasn't that big of an issue at that time.

During this time, Opie and Jimmy were on the air doing *their* show, which was *my* show. I didn't want to listen, but I kind of had to listen. I didn't listen live. Someone would say, "Opie and Jimmy were talking about you today." I'd get the clip just to see what they were saying. It's really difficult to listen to a show you were just on talking about things that concern you. I knew exactly what I would have said on air and knew just how much fun I could have been having if I'd been part of it.

I saw Opie miss so many opportunities. I would be thinking, "He could have plowed on Jimmy after saying that." I heard Opie say, "Ya know, this is a hard situation for us too. We don't know what we're doing right now, and we have to regroup." Just "me me me," of course, making himself the victim. He said, "Whatever Anthony does, we wish him the best." All bullshit. He was just saying that to make himself seem sympathetic to the listeners.

I'll reiterate: I would have gone to the big bosses and at least bluffed, saying, "You can't fire Anthony and break up the *O and A* show. This is our show, and we've been doing it for twenty years. If you're going to fire him, I'm going to have to leave. I'm not doing the show without him or re-signing my contract." Then see what they did. If they went, "Alright, take it easy," then I would have gone, "On second thought, fuck Anthony." I honestly know he made zero effort. I imagine that from the time I was fired, not a word came out of his mouth to defend me or try to get me back. I don't know how successful he would have been doing it, but at least he could have given it a fucking try.

It took a long time for me to get over being fired from Sirius. I had a lot of resentment, and for some people I still do. I have this overall resentment of the climate out there with these social justice warriors and hypocrites who are the reason I'm not working for Sirius and the *O&A* show anymore. At the time, I refused to put any of the blame on myself. I do now, to a point, but I still believe that a few years prior, I wouldn't have been fired. I think it was a timing issue and that this whole holier-than-now morality and racial sensitivity bullshit came into play. This along with the fact that I'm pretty sure Opie had been bad-mouthing me to the bosses for a while (I can't prove it). I had seen him to do it to other people, and because of this I can speculate that he did the same to me.

He would talk shit about one of our staff members to the bosses repeatedly. Then they would eventually come back to Opie and say, "We've found a replacement for that guy who's been an issue on your staff. We can fire him now." Opie would then say, "Hold on, don't fire him yet." He then would actually go to the guy he had single-handedly put in this position and tell this person that he had saved him from being fired. The guy would be like, "Thank you!" This gave him some power over that person working for us.

When I first started doing my live-stream podcast, it was similar to jocks first getting a gig on satellite radio. It was some type of radio jail. It was like being exiled to an island that you were supposed to go live out the rest of your broadcasting life on. I was coming from a big show on satellite radio to being relegated to a studio in my basement doing a podcast. It didn't look good, but the commute was amazing. I know it looked like a big step down and that I was essentially treading water to get something going. In many respects, that was true. I was trying to stay relevant in the eyes and ears of the listeners until something else clicked.

I had to keep my name out there, doing what I was doing, and this seemed like the best way. I never imagined what it would turn into. That said, I did understand that for someone like myself who has something to say to an audience, this was the future. I can't get fired, and I don't have anyone dictating what I can or can't say. Live-streaming podcasts like mine, with visuals, are the best thing to ever happen to broadcasting. If you don't like what I'm saying or something else about my show, then you can stop subscribing. It's that simple.

My podcast was pretty well received from the beginning. I watch some of the earlier shows now and get some douche chills. My whole career had been with radio, and a visual medium was a completely different animal. It was a learning process. There were even logistical concerns like how big I should be on the screen in relation to the set. That was something we had to work out. At first, I was this tiny figure at the bottom of the screen in what looked like this giant complex with a CGI background. Then we had some guys who worked for networks come in and tell us what we had to do. They flushed all that technical visual stuff out and got us up and running. Then we started incorporating simple things like lighting and a teleprompter so I could read commercials or anything I wanted to say verbatim.

We were up and running, and it was time for me to show up and make two hours funny and entertaining. The bottom line was, "Go ahead and entertain us, motherfucker!" I now had to go in on a daily basis and hope to have a fun show. I think I did okay. It was obvious for a while in the beginning that I was uncomfortable, but I think I just really hit my stride during the past year. I'm now finally at ease hosting my own show. Before, it felt like I was a panelist or a guest.

Even though there were other guests with me, I didn't feel like I was the host, and the show would get away from me. It was sometimes people talking without my having the ability to rein them in. I'm now extremely confident and comfortable hosting the show. It took time. I never stop learning. I'm continually finding myself in situations that, quite frankly, I don't know what to do about until I do it. Sometimes I have guests with two polar-opposite viewpoints verbally assaulting each other, and I have to make an executive decision about how to mediate.

What I come up with isn't always easy or fair. I go with whatever my gut says, and it's authentic. I feel if there's validity to what I do, then it will always end up being okay.

My podcast studio, as I've said, was in the basement of my house. It wasn't a big studio space. When I had guests, I liked to try to get out of the studio into my bar area and set cameras up there. It was cool, creating the vibe that my guests and I were hanging out in a bar, which is exactly what we were doing. Colin Quinn, Robert Kelly, and Jim Norton would come over and we'd do shows like that. That worked and was a lot of fun too. We had a couple of shows inside my home's movie theater; I'd play a movie and do a *Mystery Science Theater 3000* type of show. We were experimenting a bit, and I knew it would take time. I was always hopeful my audience members would hang in there, and they did. I didn't want them comparing the beginning of *The Anthony Cumia Show* to the *Opie and Anthony* show. That wouldn't be fair. That was three guys who were so comfortable and polished, and my podcast required a learning curve for me to get to where I inevitably needed to be.

Of course, I had some fans say it was a clusterfuck and "You need Opie," "Get a co-host," and "You should quit." These comments would affect me. They always did, even during my early days with Opie. Anytime you get negative comments, it affects you. I'm not impervious to things people say. I wish I were, but sometimes it's good motivation. I could read twenty great comments and the one negative one will be what I think about. During this vulnerable time of launching this new show, it was even more difficult. I just was driven to keep moving forward. It's not like I had a choice.

Within the first few months, we also decided to start our own network and produce other podcasts. We formed the Compound Media company to create and produce new shows with original talent. One thing Compound will always abide by is never telling people they can't touch on a certain topic, like race, sex, or religion. I'll let them go as far as they want to go with these taboo topics. They can do whatever they want, and the next show might be squeaky clean. There's no correlation between shows about how much respect one person gets. One show might be doing goofy shit, and another might be a legitimate political talk show. I just want shows where people can speak freely, and that doesn't happen with any other form of broadcasting.

One of the first shows we started producing was *Legion of Skanks*, with Luis J. Gomez, Dave Smith, and Big Jay Oakerson. One of their gimmicks is having a live audience around them that's constantly smoking weed. The only thing is, my studio is in my house. They'd come over with their fans, otherwise known as their "Legion of Skanks." I now have these three guys doing the show with their fans in my basement. When the show was over one time, these fucking skanks decided it was okay to take a dip in my pool. I was like, "Sure! While you're at it, why don't you come in and take a shower and dry off while I get you something to eat?" Jesus!

We also signed up Gavin McInnes. Gavin would come out to Roslyn to do my show, and he'd be pretty hammered and come upstairs. I'd be on my couch watching TV, and he'd sit down and we'd talk for three or four hours. It was great, but there were some nights when maybe I didn't want to talk for three hours. My personal life and professional show were starting to overlap. It was becoming a problem and an encroachment on my personal space.

It was time to look for new digs. Keith and I found a space in Midtown Manhattan, which we set up and designed as a state-of-the-art podcast live-streaming studio.

CHAPTER 25

My Second-Worst Mistake

I LOVE WOMEN, BUT DAMMIT if relationships haven't kicked my ass.
In March 2014, Mindy Kaling was a guest on the show. Dani Brand, who was like a kid sister to Jimmy and is the daughter of the Stress Factory comedy club owner, was a fan of Mindy and came to the studio to see the interview. Dani and I had met a couple of times prior to this throughout the years, starting back when she was in high school. She was around twenty-six at this time.

During the interview with Mindy, Dani and I would exchange glances. After the show, I asked for her number, and soon after, we hit the town for some drinks.

One thing led to another, and we started to hook up. As I mentioned, at this time in my life I wasn't looking for a steady relationship. Dani certainly wasn't my girlfriend. I wasn't looking for her to be faithful to me, and I didn't expect to be faithful to her.

When I started doing the internet show after I was fired from Sirius, she would be at my house, and my staff and Dani didn't get along at all. She wouldn't shut the fuck up and would come down to the basement during my show making all kinds of noise. She'd purposely be distracting by moving things and coming up to the glass of the sound studio. She would even fuck with my guests while they were being interviewed. She was extremely volatile and knew how to push buttons. Keith practically wanted to kill her, and his wife, Angela, couldn't stand her.

It got to the point where Keith asked me to make sure Dani didn't even come downstairs while we were taping. I then told her, "You can't come down when we're taping the show." Dani's typical reaction was, "Fuck that, fuck you, and fuck your show!" A real princess.

It was constantly like this with her. I should have known better, but believe it or not, it went on like this for a while. We were off-again on-again until we finally agreed to call it quits. It was September 2015 when I officially told her she needed to leave me and my house. I'd had enough of her bullshit and needed her out of my life. At this point, everyone knew I had grown to hate her.

Dani started crying, "I have nowhere to go." I said, "Alright, you can stay at my apartment in Manhattan until you find a place." Even though she'd be staying at my place, I made it very clear to her that we were no longer dating.

Thanksgiving rolled around, and she was still living at my apartment. I didn't really care, because "out of sight, out of mind." She called me up during the holiday season and said, "My family hates me, and I've got nowhere to go." I said, "Alright, you can come to my aunt and uncle's with me for Thanksgiving." I felt bad for her, the dumb fuck that I am.

Even Thanksgiving night we fought, and I sent her right back to the apartment.

Then came December and she was still living rent-free in my apartment. She asked, "Do you want to go out for dinner?" I was thinking, "Alright, why not? Completely platonic—what's the harm?"

We went out to dinner on Long Island and back to my house in Roslyn. She just went into crazy beast mode, saying, "Who's the girl on the phone? Who are you fucking now?" Just pushing the buttons again.

I was trying to de-escalate but found myself yelling at her in response to her constant badgering. I needed to cool the situation down. I told Dani she had to go back to my apartment. I dialed the car service to come pick her up and take her back to the city. The car showed up and she said, "I'm not going anywhere!"

I was now begging her to leave the house. If I knew then what I know now, I would have jumped in that car and gone to my apartment to sleep.

The car service driver was asking me, "What's going on?" He must have been sitting outside my home already for fifteen minutes, and I had to pay him to just drive away empty. Dani just wouldn't leave the fucking house. She kept going on and on, questioning me, "Who are you fucking? Let me see your phone!" She started grabbing my phone.

She began streaming our arguments over the internet on Periscope to a social media audience. Now we were just screaming at each other.

The cops showed up at my house. At this point, nothing had been done except for her throwing shit. I told them, "There's no problem here other than she's a little twisted. We're okay." The police then left.

Dani started kicking things into high gear. She was obsessed with seeing my phone to see who I'd been texting. She then pulled my phone from my hand and smashed it on the floor.

I reciprocated by smashing her phone, but not before she tried to incriminate me by fabricating my slapping her. You can clearly see her own hand hitting herself and her saying, "Stop hitting me." You can hear me from my kitchen saying, "I'm not hitting you!" So that went out on Periscope. I did not and would not hit her or any female.

I came into the living room and told her to say I hadn't been hitting her. She then slapped me on my ear with an open hand. It caused a loud ringing sound that hurt like a motherfucker.

I instantly retorted by biting her hand between her thumb and her pointer finger. I didn't break the skin; it was just hard enough to make a bruise.

She wanted to run to the neighbor's house to call the police. I was trying to call the car service again, because I wanted her out. She started pulling the landline phone wires out of the wall—drunk off her ass, vindictive, rejected, and just insane.

I didn't want her running through the neighborhood drunk. I also didn't want the police coming back and possibly arresting me based on her false allegations. I just wanted this to settle down.

She ran out of my house, and there was little I could do. My surveillance cameras caught all of the outside action. She later said in the police report that I had grabbed her by the hair and dragged her back into the house. This clearly wasn't the case.

This went on for literally hours. Then it was morning, with the sun coming up, and I said, "Let's get in the truck and go to the Apple Store. I'll buy two new phones and we'll call this a fucking day. You can go back to the apartment and that's it."

Again, "Fuck this! Fuck you!"

I told her, "Well, I'm going to the Apple Store, and you can stay here."

Another false allegation she made was that I didn't let her leave my home on her own. Really? I was begging her to leave. Meanwhile, in reality, I was walking out the door by myself to get a new phone and she came running out and jumped into my truck. Hey, who doesn't want a new iPhone? Once again, this was all verified by my outside video surveillance cameras.

We went to the Apple Store and bought two new phones. There was no pleading for her life at the store, no "this man is beating me and holding me hostage in his house." The only words out of her mouth were, "I think we should get cases and more storage space."

We got back into the car and drove back to the house. Welcoming me home were four cop cars and eight officers waiting for us. Clueless me, I was looking at this and thinking, "I wonder what's going on? What is this about?"

I got out of the car, and one cop asked me, "Where were you? Was there a fight? Did you hit each other?"

A female officer whisked Dani away to speak with her inside the house. I was talking to the other cops on my porch.

Fifteen minutes later the female cop came out with Dani, and they walked right by us and got into a police car. A male officer came over to me and said, "Turn around, you're under arrest."

Whatever was discussed inside my house was enough to get me arrested. She showed the bruise on her hand and said that I had stomped on her hand while she was on the ground. She also stated that I had kicked her in the ribs and strangled her against the door. I was thinking, "What the fuck?" This was beyond me; I felt like I was in some kind of bizarro world where strange fiction was becoming reality.

I was hauled away in cuffs because this fucking bitch had said I had done her harm—never mentioning that she had hit me on the side of my head, kicked me, and pulled my hair during the course of the night when I had desperately been pleading for her to go to my apartment that I was letting her stay at rent-free.

She then went right back to my apartment and stayed there another five months. I couldn't throw her out at that point, if you can believe it.

I wanted to see the video from my surveillance cameras. Keith told me, "The cops took the hard drive." There were a bunch of wires in my basement that used to be screwed into a hard drive, and now there was no hard drive. The police said, "We don't have it. No one has it."

The district attorney assigned to my case was a man-hating woman, who was actually fired for withholding evidence on a domestic abuse case a couple of months after my case was settled.

My surveillance footage would have proven that Dani was lying, and it disappeared. Coincidence? Of course not! Coincidence that this same lady was fired a couple of months later for doing the same thing to another poor bastard? Do the math.

It was the biggest fucking I've gotten since my divorce case. Anytime I step into a court, it's going to be a big ass-fucking for me. I settled for a harassment violation, which is essentially a ticket. But all of my guns were taken away, and my pistol permit was revoked.

I lost my Second Amendment right when some girl made bullshit allegations against me. That's for two years. Then after two years I have to start all over again trying to convince people that I'm competent to bear arms. I'm a gun enthusiast. I like target shooting and collecting. This was all taken away because some insecure chick felt vindictive about my being done with her. I've heard she has moved to San Diego. A different country would be better, but I'll take it.

I decided to settle my case and take a plea bargain. I could have gone to trial and won. There was also a chance I could have lost and gone to jail. Even though I was innocent, I wasn't going to risk it. It gave me an honest look at how our legal system really works, and it has nothing to do with justice. It's all about the money.

Part of my plea bargain was that I had to attend a domestic abuse course and then rehab for alcohol.

I started with the domestic abuse class, which was in Jericho, Long Island. I met privately with a woman in her office. She would put a videotape into a VCR that showed the proper way to handle domestic situations. Some of them were hilarious. I literally had to bite my tongue to curtail my laughter.

These videos showed what was not the right way to relate to or treat women by showing footage of Andrew "Dice" Clay's act and a segment of a film featuring Artie Lange. It's not good when you're watching a video of what not to do with women, and your friends are the actual people used as the examples.

She knew who I was and what I did for a living. I was doing my show one day, and the next day I went in for my class. I noticed she was very cold to me. She sat me down and said, "I don't know if I can treat you anymore." I was like, "What happened? I need this! I can't get thrown out the course!"

She said, "I watched your show yesterday, and you said something about when rape isn't rape." I'm thinking, "Of all the fucking breaks! She had to hear this show."

I said, "There's rapey rape and rapedy rape rape. See, there's rapey rape when a guy crawls through a window and beats a girl up. Then he rapes her. The girl's like, 'Oh my God, who was that?' They call the police. Then there's rapedy rapey rape, which is when a friend comes over and maybe you regret it the next day. You call it rape but it's more regret."

This woman was livid. To her, if I were to say, "That's a nice dress you're wearing," that would be just about rape.

I now had to convince her that this was just a show and it was a bit, that it wasn't really me. Do you think I would really say something like that? It's show business. *Seinfeld* was named after Jerry Seinfeld, but that isn't Jerry Seinfeld on the show. It's a character he's playing. On *The Anthony Cumia Show*, I'm playing a character. I was dancing like a motherfucker trying to convince this woman to continue working with me: "You're really helping me! I've come so far!"

For the next month, I really had to watch what I said on my show. I knew that at any moment she could be listening and that any one thing I said could have been the one that got me thrown out of class. Getting thrown out of a court-appointed domestic violence class is never good.

I'd say by the second week, I stopped fantasizing about smacking the shit out of my teacher. Kidding. It worked out well, and she gave me exemplary marks and I left her with no marks. I guess the class really did work.

CHAPTER 26

Rehab

I HAD TO GO TO a thirty-day rehab, which really infuriated me. I actually volunteered to go, because my lawyer said, "If you volunteer, it looks a lot better than if it's court-appointed."

I originally thought it would be a class similar to the domestic violence one I had just finished. I'd go twice a week, and that would be it. Little did I know I'd be going to Fort Lauderdale, Florida, for a fucking month!

Under grave protest I went. I didn't drink for four days prior to flying out there. I actually watched rehab movies like *28 Days* and *Clean and Sober* to prep. I never had been to rehab and didn't know what the fuck it would entail.

I knew I didn't have a drinking problem. It wasn't drinking that had gotten me into this situation. Perhaps I would have made better decisions if I hadn't been drinking that night. It was being a dummy and feeling sorry for a lying piece of shit that had gotten me into the situation I was currently in.

When I first got there, I had to go to the detox center for three or four days. I don't drink enough even on a binge to warrant detoxing, and I already hadn't had a drink in four days.

This place was filled with hardcore drug addicts and alcoholics who were going through some serious DTs. They told me I'd have to be medicated twice a day and I'd have to go up to the window where they'd distribute medication.

Medication? What the fuck? I went to the window and said, "I'm supposed to get medicine? What is this?"

They said, "Xanax. When you're coming off alcohol, we don't want you to have a seizure. So we give you Xanax."

I told them, "I don't need anything. I'm fine. I haven't drank in four days. Even before that I wasn't drinking a lot."

"Nope, you have to take them. It's the law," they told me.

I said, "Alright. Give me it." I popped the Xanax, and ten minutes later I was on the couch in the day room completely fucked up on a different planet. My eyes were at half-mast, my mouth was hanging open, and I was humming.

The Xanax buzz was awesome. I was feeling great. I was sitting there thinking, "This is my first day in rehab? This makes no sense to me at all. I come here completely sober, and now I'm wasted on Xanax. Maybe I was wrong about rehab?"

I had four days of this, and then they shipped me off to the rehab center. It was April and eighty-five degrees down there. The place had a pool and was right on the beach. It was fucking amazing!

After three days they made me president of the group. I was the one who handed out the work details to the other patients. I never had to do anything! I never lifted a finger! And I'd never been president of anything before this!

They would give everyone multiple assignments every day, but I had to do only one. I'd see people with the books working things out. I only had to show the differences between me and the on-air me—how I presented myself to people in real life and how I presented myself to my audience.

In real life, I was "generous, kind, and taciturn." Then the on-air me was "an asshole, brutal, and misogynistic."

It was like I was five years old and turning in my school project. And that's all I turned in.

I spent the rest of my time in the pool flirting with the girls, eating, and smoking a vape. To fit in at rehab, you have to have smoke coming out of your face. Everyone smoked cigarettes there. It ended up being kinda fun. Some people would leave, and new drunks and addicts would replace them. It was an interesting stay.

Artie had gone to the same rehab and recommended it. Artie Lange recommending a rehab facility is like Gordon Ramsay recommending a new restaurant. You're gonna listen!

I had a roommate while I was there. My first roommate was a by-the-book kind of patient. A hardcore alcoholic who could have blackouts and murder someone without knowing it. Perfect. Just the guy I wanted sleeping next to me.

The next roommate was great! He was a heroin addict from Oklahoma who shared my same sick sense of humor. He and I ran that place!

I would take nightly trips to AA meetings. I literally had thirty AA meetings. I would just sit there pissed, looking at the signs that said things like, "One day at a time." I never felt like I belonged there and couldn't jibe with the program. People would get up and tell their stories, and I'd be thinking, "I don't even have one of these." Step number one is realizing that you have a problem and that your life is out of control because of alcohol. I was like, "No. I've had some out-of-control moments because of booze. Maybe I wasn't thinking at the time? I'm not gonna say my life is out of control. My life is pretty good." I would then see these people telling stories such as, "I dropped a gallon of vodka on the bathroom floor, and I sucked it up with a straw." Yeah, that's not me.

I served my thirty days and didn't care that there wasn't any booze or beer. It didn't bother me. Someone drove me to the airport and said the obligatory stuff: "If you need anything, here's my number. Make sure you get to meetings and get a sponsor. We're gonna text you and check in." I said, "Thank you." I then proceeded to walk into the airport and directly to the President's Club bar and ordered a beer. I popped the top on an ice-cold Bud, and I saw the little bit of vapor that comes out when you crack it open. I blew it off. I wanted it to be great, and it was. It was one of the best beers I ever had. The whole plane ride back, I was indulging in Bloody Marys. I came back to LaGuardia Airport from my month in rehab hammered. Mission accomplished.

CHAPTER 27

Look at My Weiner

I**T WAS THE SUMMER** of 2011 and I was a guest on the Fox News show *Red Eye*, hosted by Greg Gutfeld. After the show, Greg and I, along with the other guests on the panel and the show's producers, went out to a bar called Langan's on 47th Street. The guys who work at these news talk shows know how to fucking drink! I've never seen people in any industry who drink more than these guys. Possibly Wall Street suits, but media guys are right there.

Greg told me, "Ann Coulter is on her way down with Andrew Breitbart." I had never met Andrew before and was excited. At this time, Andrew was the only guy aside from Weiner to possess the infamous Weiner picture.

The news had been showing pictures of Anthony Weiner flexing in a mirror that he had accidentally sent out over Twitter and then quickly deleted. The money shot was this dick pic. Everyone was like, "Where is this dick pic? Does anyone have the dick pic?" Andrew Breitbart had it on his phone, and he couldn't show it to enough people. He was showing this dick pic to everybody!

All I was thinking was, "How can I get publicity for the *Opie and Anthony* show with this picture?" I asked Andrew if he could come on our show the next day, and he agreed to do it.

The next morning, he was at our studio. Andrew was a staunch conservative. A right-wing-leaning guy. Our other guest that day was the actor Vincent D'Onofrio, who is a bleeding-heart liberal. The two had never met but knew each other by reputation and knew they had polar-opposite political views. They hated each other. That added a great dynamic to the show as well. Andrew sat down and they were cordial, but they took little snips at each other's political ideologies.

We then started talking to Andrew about the Anthony Weiner dick pic. Understand, this was the story that everyone was buzzing about— the hottest topic on every talk show and news program at the time.

Andrew started to pass his phone around the room for everyone to see. Again, he just couldn't show this to enough people. This was his "check this out, I have this and no one else does" kind of thing.

I had my video-conferencing Paltalk on live, as I did every show. The Paltalk camera was on me, and as the phone was going around I looked at the picture and started laughing. It was then my turn to pass it to Opie. I turned Andrew's phone around so that the picture was facing the Paltalk camera that was normally capturing me doing the show. I purposely held it there for a little while, knowing that everyone watching was screen-capturing this image and getting the dick picture of Anthony Weiner. I then passed Opie the phone, and it made its way back to Andrew.

After the show, I noticed that everyone was posting their screen-cap image. People were now texting it to me. I now had the Anthony Weiner dick pic!

Opie and I both put the picture out there on social media with our names firmly attached to it.

The news broke and stations everywhere started showing the picture. Obviously, it had to be pixelated, but nonetheless it was everywhere with our names attached. We received major publicity because of this, which was exactly the plan.

Andrew Breitbart texted me, and he was fucking pissed. This was his baby. He said, "I can't believe you betrayed my trust like that. I needed to have that picture to get other things!" He asked why I'd done it.

I texted back, "I'm sorry."

It makes me think of that story about the scorpion and the frog. The frog needs to get across the river, and the scorpion asks for a ride. The frog's like, "You're not gonna sting me, right?" The scorpion's like, "No, why would I sting you? Then we'd both drown." "Alright, get on." And they go across the river. In the middle of the river, the scorpion stings the frog, and the frog asks, "Why the fuck did you do that? Now we're both gonna die." "Because I'm a scorpion. That's what I do."

Because I'm a radio guy! That's why I did it! For radio personalities, publicity is the number-one goal. Getting more people to hear your name, regardless of what it's attached to, is your goal on a daily basis. Getting them to talk about you. Even with the worst firing catastrophes Opie and I had, our first thought was, "Cool, we got some press."

I felt bad about what I did to Andrew. At the same time, I was thinking, "You were the one who handed it to us." It was a shitty thing to do, but again I had that shock jock mindset. I was the scorpion.

I don't even know if Anthony Weiner knew or realized we were the ones who released the photo publicly.

A couple of years ago, Keith the cop, my executive producer, had a meeting with Weiner. We considered having him join our Compound Media company and giving him his own show. They had a good meeting, which turned into a second meeting with Keith and me.

This took place during a presidential campaign. Weiner was all over the news because of the Hillary Clinton emails that had ended up on his computer. He walked into the restaurant incognito, with a hat and sunglasses on.

It was pretty hilarious that years after the dick pic, he was now interviewing with me hoping to do a show. He was really nice, and I certainly didn't mention anything regarding the infamous photo. I'm not sure to this day whether he knows I was the one who leaked the image that was the catalyst for his downfall.

He started mentioning things like, "I was talking to ABC Radio, and they have some interest."

I was thinking, "No you don't. ABC is owned by Disney. They don't want someone who sent a photo of his boner to a teenage girl. Don't try to bargain with lies." I knew that no one wanted this guy.

We were psyched about having him on Compound Media, until he was sentenced to jail.

When he gets out, if he wants a job, he's got it. We're like that old loan company: when everyone else says no, we say yes!

Keith and I have been thinking we could use a liberal voice on our network. Even if it is Anthony Weiner. Actually, even better if it is Anthony Weiner embroiled in controversy. That's what we're about. We are so pro freedom of speech, why not let the guy talk? If he has something to say, I don't care what he did. He still has the right to express his opinions.

When he's done being incarcerated, he's most likely fucked. Who's going to hire someone who was sending illicit sexual material to a minor? This guy! Talk about second chances. Anthony Cumia will give you a third, fourth, and fifth chance. We'll see.

CHAPTER 28

To Be or Not to Be—Artie

WHEN I STARTED DOING my live podcast, it was just me. It was low-rent, just Keith and me running things, and we eventually built *The Anthony Cumia Show* into a success. It began thriving once we moved to our current Midtown Manhattan studio.

We started getting some feedback from people saying, "Hey, Anthony, have you ever considered having a co-host?"

I had never really given that thought any serious consideration. Every so often I'd think, "That person was really fun to do the show with." But it was never, "Oh shit, I need a co-host."

I was with Opie for two decades. Getting a co-host right when I started the podcast would have been like getting divorced and getting remarried right away. I was enjoying my independence and also finally really comfortable hosting on my own. I liked being able to say and do whatever the fuck I wanted, when I wanted. It's good to be the king! It was working very well by myself.

The Anthony Cumia Show and the *Opie and Anthony* show are like night and day. The podcast is news-based and has a lot of conservative stuff. Not like Sean Hannity's or Russ Limbaugh's show. It has my political take with my humor. I had no intention of making it some staunch political program. That said, I realized my show was pretty one-sided politically, and I started seeing the value in getting another voice to balance things out. Someone who might have a different ideology or give me some feedback. Then I had to start thinking, who? This person would come on board and share my show with me the entire time. It wouldn't be just for a day. It would be every day. Keith and I had thought about it and just couldn't come up with anyone who could be that person.

I had been offered the opportunity to be a guest on *The Artie Lange Show*. It was a recorded podcast he was doing in Hoboken, New Jersey. He would do it once or twice a week from the kitchen in his apartment. I was actually pretty excited about going over there and checking out what his deal was. I had heard some of his shows, and they were very funny. I was honored to be asked to do it after all the shit we'd had in the past between *The Howard Stern Show* and the *Opie and Anthony* show. It was kind of weird even being in the same room with him talking to him. Not that I had any issues with him, or that he had any with me. It's just one of those things, that the two shows had a history.

Keith and I took the ferry over to Hoboken. Artie has this beautiful apartment right on the Hudson River overlooking the Manhattan skyline, but it resembled a fraternity house.

Artie was hilarious; he came out right away making excuses for the decor. "I'm having some work done." "They're painting the walls." "I had a mold problem and they fixed it but I still need paint." "I'm getting crown molding." He was saying all this stuff, and I was thinking, "Yeah, a college kid lives here." I was cracking up, and again, everything he said was hilariously funny. The guy is just hysterical.

Then it was time to actually record his show, and we sat down at his dining room table. We fired up the microphones and instantly had a rapport. When we started talking about whatever it was that first time on his show, we both knew how to talk to each other without stepping on each other. We both knew how to make a story funny and how to complement each other. It was just amazingly easy for the two of us to do a show.

On the ferry ride back to Manhattan, Keith and I started talking. "Could you imagine Artie and me doing a show?" I asked him. It would be amazing. Keith is the go-getter. I'm the guy who would have let it stay right there and never acted on it. Keith liked the idea and started making calls to Artie and his people. Artie was really psyched about the idea of doing it, but with all the other people involved and Artie's having issues with drugs, there was always a problem. We just couldn't make it work out.

We were still looking for other potential prospects, to no avail. Nobody else created that instant rapport that Artie and I had had. Artie then came on and did my show, and I went back to Hoboken to do his show a couple of times. There was one occasion when I made the trek to do his show and got to his place and he wasn't there. It's not like he was meeting me somewhere at a studio. I got over there and Dan, his friend and producer, said, "Yeah, Artie had to leave." I was like, "Leave? What? We're scheduled to tape the show here." "Here" being his own apartment! How can you be MIA from your own place? Well, if anyone can, it would be Artie.

I then got back on the ferry with Keith, and we started thinking it would be really great to have Artie as a co-host, but was this guy at all dependable? He couldn't even make it to his own show at his house! How the fuck was he going to make it to our studio?

Nonetheless, as time went on, Keith still made inquiries about Artie, and finally we were all on the same page. Artie had a problem with his podcast and wasn't going to continue doing it.

We decided it would be a good idea to merge talents and make this happen. I had worked with him only four times but had seen enough to know we were a good fit. I also saw him at Carolines on Broadway when he did Gilbert Gottfried's show as a guest. It was one of the funniest shows I've ever seen. They were talking about old movies and TV shows. Gilbert was referencing movies from the thirties, and Artie was talking about his family. I was watching with Keith and said, "This guy is just fucking amazingly hilarious."

Everything got worked out contractually to have Artie on board officially with Compound Media. We were thinking about what the logo for Artie and Anthony should be. AA is kind of ironic, to say the least.

As far as pictures go, we're not the most attractive guys in entertainment, let alone radio. We're not kids anymore, and we've been through the mill more than a few times. The photos certainly weren't going to be glamour shots! We decided it would be funny if we used our mug shots. I had one mug shot from the Dani episode, and Artie had a lot of mug shots! He had mug shots from various states and even from France. The guy has a mug shot from France! Artie went with the one he had from Miami. When he was arrested and being processed for booking, he was smiling. He looks like he was having a great time. He said that's because he still thought he was at the party. It's one of the greatest mug shots of all time. It could be his head shot.

We were now down to the wire of doing our first show together as *The Artie and Anthony Show*. Now mind you, Artie and I had never spoken to each other except for before and after the shows we had done. We'd never sat down and had a conversation about what the show would be or what our dreams or aspirations were. I knew nothing about him whatsoever in regard to him as a person and what we were going to be doing on the show together.

We decided not to tell our audience who my new co-host was going to be. We made it into a teaser bit. Over the course of time, we told people we were going to have a co-host and would let everyone speculate about who it was going to be. Some people thought it was going to be Jim Norton, who would have been amazing but was under contract to Sirius XM and couldn't do it. Others actually thought it was going to be Opie, who had recently been fired. That was hilarious—like I would have wanted to jump back into that frying pan!

On Monday, August 21, 2017, we announced the new co-host. There was a video that opened the show, and it included Ron Bennington, Rich Vos, Nick Di Paolo, Bob Kelly, Bobo, and Jim Norton as Chip Chipperson. We then narrowed down the potential candidates for the job in the studio, which included Ron, Jimmy, and finally Artie Lange, who came fashionably late his first day on the job. Typical Artie—we wanted to announce the guy, and he wasn't even there! He did make it in, and it actually helped build the excitement when we did declare it was indeed him.

Artie's debut was effortless. It was as if we'd been working together for years. I think it was better that we didn't have any preliminary dinner meetings or discussions on the format. He's a pro and a perfect fit for the show.

We fell right into a natural rhythm with each other. Having been on *The Howard Stern Show* and being the joke guy filling in for Jackie Martling was the greatest grooming possible for being a beast behind the mic. The difference between Artie and Jackie is that Artie is a lot more vocal. Jackie wrote a lot of stuff to feed Howard, and Artie would just say it. Artie is just like one of your best friends, a guy you'd hang out at a bar with.

It's not an act. He's just a lovable, big, funny guy. It comes across whenever he does anything. I honestly think that's the only reason he still has friends! We've all dealt with Artie's issues, some people for a lot longer than others. I was still pretty new to the whole thing when Artie came on board. I remember being at the Comedy Cellar in NYC and Dave Attell, who had been a great friend of Artie's for many years, came up to me saying, "Welcome to the world of Artie Lange: the late-night phone calls, the not showing up, and the 'I love you/you're an asshole!'"

I was kind of bewildered at first, but it didn't take long for me to be like, "Oh, this is how it is." That demon of chemical dependency makes people give up on their family, friends, and career. I was well aware of this before making my decision to have Artie as my co-host. Judd Apatow is also someone well aware of it, and he actually wrote it into the storyline of the HBO show *Crashing*. It's no secret and that's the best part of it. It's not somebody trying to hide an addiction. It's someone we all know who has an addiction, and we're not enabling it. We're just keeping the guy alive.

Artie goes through the highs and the lows of addiction. One thing I have to say, when he gets behind that mic, goddamn is that guy funny, sharp, and quick. I really can't imagine sitting there doing the show with any other co-host at this point. I would feel like I'd be the one carrying the show again, like Jimmy and I carried the *O&A* show for so many years. I don't want to be in that position anymore. It's not ever like that with Artie. Every so often, especially if you're doing a show alone, you reach a point where you're discussing something and you want to change subjects. It might be an awkward segue, and you don't know quite how to do it. There might be some dead air. Artie innately knows how to pick up on that and fill it up. Not many people know how to do that. If there's silence, it was meant to be there. A dramatic pause or taking a beat before the punch line. Artie is on the greatest radio show ever and knows how to do it like it's an involuntary reflex.

Working with Artie has been great! It has definitely changed the show's dynamic completely. I like the fact that I'm not so obsessed about politics. Artie has added a lot more laughter, making fun of shit and goofing on our friends and guests the whole way through.

It's not always easy for guests to be sandwiched between Artie and me. Sometimes I actually feel bad for them. Artie and I will be riffing back and forth like a furious fast-paced tennis volley. The guest in between us is like a ball boy just waiting to run in when it's over to pick up the tennis ball and get it out of the way for us to continue playing. It's a really tough seat to be in.

Artie's attendance hasn't been the most consistent, due to his personal issues. If this were high school, he would be in danger of being left back a grade. I knew this going into it, and quite frankly it's not a problem for me whatsoever. If he's there, great, and if he's not, it's okay. I'm fortunately very comfortable running the show solo.

There have been a few times since we've been a team show when Artie was on drugs. He was not well. There's an overtly noticeable difference between Artie when he's sober and when he's high. The most discernible thing is that he doesn't have the focus when he's high. He's not able to really zero in on a topic and stick with it. I think sometimes he wanted to distract the people who were watching from the fact that he might be high by keeping the subjects changing. But continuously talking actually magnifies the fact that he is high.

When he's sober, it's obvious. When he's not sober, it's obvious. Everyone knows, and no one is ever fooled. At the beginning, it was hard for me to tell. I guess I didn't know him well enough. Now I can absolutely tell the moment he walks in the door. When he was high, it was a lot more difficult to do the show. And it did get frustrating. I had to work extra hard to make sure the show wasn't a mess. There were some weeks that would go like that.

He went into the hospital and came back, and I realized he could do the show sober. Fortunately, he's been great and sharp as a tack on the show. I love it and it really works well. He's a super talented, funny guy who is a great yin to my yang.

Those with extraordinary talent that makes what they do seem easy are often plagued by demons. Those demons are the impetus behind what they bring to their craft. It's not fair, but that's just the way it is. I have no idea what the future will be in regard to Artie. The man was born to talk, and I'm glad it's with me.

CHAPTER 29

Just Let Me Talk

THE CLIMATE OF THE country these days makes it a very interesting time to be in any type of broadcasting. When I came up in radio in the mid-nineties, the FCC was the big bad monster. Today, political correctness has everybody in trouble. Now what group is going to get me fired?

I used to be worried just about getting a fine. The boss would come in and yell at us, saying, "You said 'pee-pee' or 'poop' too much. Here's the transcript, read it." It's embarrassing to see your name in front of bodily functions. They'd say, "You might need to pay a fine. They're going to try to litigate it." That was frightening back then. I always wondered if I might lose my job because of an FCC complaint.

Now you say something so innocent, and then the next day some group will be calling for your head, equating you with the Antichrist. Your boss will feel the pressure and fire you. You don't even know what happened, and they're ushering you out of the building because you made a joke about gay people or a woman's hairdo. It's gotten so crazy.

There is such a lack of freedom of speech in broadcasting. There's barely freedom of speech in person when you're talking in public. In broadcasting, find me one radio station on FM or AM that has a radio personality doing a free-form kind of personality-driven radio. You can't!

They don't exist anymore, because the owners of these radio stations are so scared that they will be looked at as being racist, sexist, or homophobic. They just tell their jocks to shut up, play the music, and read the liners that lead into the next song.

I thought satellite radio would give our show the luxury of freedom of speech. I certainly didn't think I would be fired for saying something on social media that had nothing to do with the place that I worked at. That's an interesting take. I knew there was a problem in the business when I got fired for tweeting things off the air, completely detached from Sirius XM radio. When I was fired, I was like, "Okay, this is not good."

When I then started *The Anthony Cumia Show*, I realized I could do and say whatever the fuck I wanted. It was the first time in any type of broadcast I had been involved with that I had absolutely no restrictions on what I could do and say. It was really amazing and liberating.

The oddest part of the whole thing is that I didn't take advantage of it the way I thought I would. In the month that it took us to gear up after I was fired till the time that we started the internet show, everybody was talking about how I would be able to do the Fifty-Five Gallon Drum Challenge again! In that one, we would shove broads into a barrel and drop shit on them. And I was gonna be able to do cherry darts again—throwing cherries into girls' assholes. I initially was thinking, "Yeah I'll be able to do all that!" But when push came to shove, I felt happier and more interested in just talking.

I don't know why we were so compelled to do those stunts during our shock jock years with the *O&A* show. I'm not blaming Opie for anything, but I honestly think it was his way of not having a discussion, actually exchanging ideas and debating topics. It was a lot easier to have a woman shoot eggs out of her pussy than it was for him to discuss current events and politics.

I was more comfortable just talking. I found that I could be funny, compelling, and interesting to the listeners without having to have this spoiled, jumping around, banging on pots and pans, "look at me" thing. That's what we did on the *Opie and Anthony* show throughout our career.

I put some value on the fact that we got publicity from it. If we did something outrageous, sometimes the news stations would pick up on it. Mostly they wouldn't. Sure, these sophomoric vulgar gags titillated our audience members, and they liked it. But I don't think it was any better than just having a conversation with your friends.

I think I matured in the actual job of being in a broadcast medium. Whether it was on the radio or doing the live-streaming show, I felt uncomfortable getting into my fifties and still doing shit like that. I came to the conclusion that relying on lowbrow gags reveals you're a one-trick pony.

My new platform definitely discusses politics. If I want the entire audience, why do I talk about politics? Why am I so right-leaning when I know I'm alienating half my audience? I think if you're preaching to an audience, you can alienate the other half. If you're having a fun discussion about what you believe in, I don't think you're driving away those who have a different viewpoint. Sure, some people won't want to listen to it. I do think the majority likes compelling, interesting conversation. That's such a rare thing these days.

Aside from Compound Media and a few other companies out there that are doing alternative media, there's nowhere you can really voice your opinion anymore. Unless it's the opinion of the one running your company. I also always consider having guests with opposing opinions.

To me, freedom of speech is the number-one right. It doesn't require any mechanism or machinery. Anyone can exercise freedom of speech at any time. I believe it's an absolute right. I'm an absolutist when it comes to the First Amendment.

If you know me, you know that social media and I have a topsy-turvy relationship. It's sort of an obsession with me, and I always end up getting royally fucked. I'm notoriously always getting in trouble on social media. I'm very open about what I say and have no filter. If I think something, it goes out there immediately before I even think of the consequences.

Social media has turned into something completely different from what it started as. The first thing I ever heard about Twitter was in the newspaper. It was a picture of a guy who had just come down a slide of an airplane that had made an emergency landing. The picture showed the guy running from the plane, and the article said the photo was taken from the guy's Twitter account. I was like, "What is this?" I then signed up for it and I started checking it out. It was mostly people posting pictures and some funny jokes. It appeared to be good-natured and harmless. It has now been bastardized and become one of the ugliest, nastiest places around, and I don't see any good coming from it. I can understand if you're in some form of show business and need to plug a gig. Then maybe. But even with that, the price to pay might be too high. "I'll be performing in Vegas next week." "Yeah, go fuck yourself! You're a hack!"

Anytime you put yourself out there, you're opening yourself up to the social media piranhas who live to seek and destroy. I don't know what business anybody has going on a public forum and just putting themselves out there to get shit on by everyone else watching. It's become so mean-spirited. The exaggerated lies that come out of it and the way the news is now distorted because of social media are staggering.

People see a headline or they watch the news with one eye and one ear, interpreting a story one way. They then post about it as if it were true, and then people run with it on a mass level. This altered reality, a fabrication, becomes the truth. It doesn't matter what the actual truth was; the new truth says something different. "This must be real, right?" No! It's not real!

A great example of this is the fiasco regarding Jon Stewart and me at the Comedy Cellar. It was nothing, but social media made it into our almost getting into fisticuffs. It made national news! The story that came out was the furthest thing from the truth.

I was at the bar with my girlfriend and Steve Grillo from *The Howard Stern Show*. Jon was with the actor-comedian Aziz Ansari at a table. Jon walked by and Steve extended his hand to Jon, introducing himself as being from *The Howard Stern Show*. Jon looked at me and I said, "Hey, Jon, how ya doing? I'm Anthony Cumia." Jon didn't accept my handshake and said, "Oh, you. I don't want to fuckin' talk to you. Fuck you, you've said nasty shit about me." I was like, "Jon, you're in the public eye and I do a radio show. Yes, I've talked about you. How long have you been in this business? That's what people do." He yelled, "Yeah, but you said shit that…" I said, "Did you hear it?" "No. I heard people say it."

It went back and forth, and we were discussing what he had heard I said about him. It wasn't anything that everyone else hasn't said about Jon Stewart: "You're a liberal and you took a liberal tack on *The Daily Show*." It was nothing big. Our interaction at the table was over before it started. He actually came around and said something like, "Alright, maybe I was a little harsh there," and we ended up shaking hands and squashing it.

This one-minute interaction got blown up into a much bigger deal because social media distorted the facts. Facebook, bloggers, and Twitter have twisted ethics rules, and when people saw posts about it, it became a "legitimate" source of news. You'd like to think the real news outlets and journalists have some real sense of integrity. I don't believe it. You'd like to believe. No one even has to fake it on social media. Probably 99 percent of what you read on there is total bullshit, and the other 1 percent is mostly bullshit. It's like when you're a kid and say a word into one kid's ear, and by the time it gets to the last kid it's a completely different word.

The only difference is that with social media, by the time the second person has a story, it's already twisted and exaggerated way out of proportion. It's a much better story if Jon and Anthony almost throw down and Anthony has to be held back from hitting Jon. But that couldn't be further from the truth. He's way too short and skinny for me to even consider fighting him. I'm not some tough guy, but I certainly wasn't worried about a fight scenario with Jon—although he did have Aziz Ansari watching his back, and I already had gotten in trouble once for allegations that I struck a woman!

Whenever I was reined in on any broadcast medium and couldn't talk about what I wanted to talk about, I felt like I was being held back.

I was angry because I knew this was within my constitutional right as an American. I've been suspended on satellite radio for things I've said or done that should have been protected by my First Amendment rights. I've been suspended on every form of social media there is, starting with Myspace and going right up to Twitter. Maybe not Instagram, because I just post pictures of my cat. I've been suspended from every other medium, and it has always made me feel permanently suspended from society.

I've never done anything that warranted being suspended. I'm not saying, "I'm going to kill you, motherfucker!" I'm not saying anyone is a piece of shit: "Fuck the Jews! Muslims need to die!" I've never said anything like that or close to that. I've been suspended for having a basic debate and discussion, voicing my viewpoints in an articulate, respectful way. I've been suspended for stating a point of view that wasn't on a par with that of the people running the social media platform.

People will say the government owes you the right to free speech, but the bosses at a company can do whatever they want. Should they be able to have that right? If I'm walking down the street and somebody prevents me from talking, they're infringing on a right. Social media platforms like Facebook and Twitter are infringing on peoples' rights when they allow one person to do something and don't allow another to do something based on nothing but ideology. That's an absolute infringement of the right to freedom of speech.

This is why Compound Media is so important. I'm not going to suspend myself. Keith cannot suspend me. Keith actually has texted me in the middle of the night saying, "You really think that's a smart tweet you just made there?" I'd review it and be like, "Eh, I don't know."

At this point in my life, with what I've gone through in broadcasting, I really feel I have the right to say whatever the fuck I want! I put together my own platform. I had to build my own medium so I wouldn't be suspended or fired. It's the only way I can have a job. As long as I have a voice and someone to listen, I will continue doing what I love most.

EPILOGUE

Twenty-plus years later and I'm still commuting to Manhattan from Long Island, or vice versa. And it's still the best time for me to reflect and dream.

I now have the good fortune to drive an insanely fast, expensive brand-new Jaguar F-Type. Every single time I sit in this car, it reminds me of my dick size.

I was recently driving back after my show to my house in Long Island, and I saw an Apollo Air Conditioning van ahead of me on the Long Island Expressway. It was the same piece of shit I used to drive when I worked there. I immediately had this impulse to catch up to it and see the guy driving it.

I could literally see, smell, and feel what it was like to be that guy driving back from some thankless shit job in NYC.

I caught up and looked out my passenger window, and I saw the driver of the van. This guy looked just miserable. He had the hat and uniform on. I have to give him major props for that, because I rarely ever wore either. I was never the company-guy type.

The driver of the van was looking out his windshield with an almost dead stare at the road. I could only imagine what was going on in his mind. I knew damn well it wasn't Apollo Air Conditioning. He had some dream, some other thing than driving that van that he rather would have been doing. I fucking empathized with this guy I didn't even know, but I did at the same time.

He and I were in such different worlds at this point. He had no idea that the guy next to him in the brand-new exotic sports car used to be him. I was that guy!

I'm not saying I'm better than this guy, because I'm not. I'm just saying I can relate, and when I saw his face, it brought me right back to where I used to be. I know that when I was sitting where he was, I wanted to be something different. The odds that someone will get out of that situation are astronomical, but I did.

This young air-conditioning guy turned his head and saw me looking at him. I gave him a nod, and he flipped me the finger. I then stomped on the gas and took off at about 120 miles per hour, never looking back—only forward, motherfucker!

ACKNOWLEDGMENTS

My FAMILY HAS ALWAYS been of the utmost importance to me and been there through the toughest times. They have supported my dreams and have been my constant boosters. This includes my mom, my brother Joe and my sister Dawn. Thanks to my father for being the inspiration for so many bits. I'm glad to have inherited his same love of comedy.

I want to recognize Opie for seeing my talent and giving me the opportunity to work in radio which forever changed my life, in the best way possible.

Thanks to Jim Norton for being a great friend and sharing my same sick, twisted sense of humor. Thank you for helping me keep my sanity during the rougher times that Opie and I endured. I appreciate the effortless comedy synergy we have riffing with each other.

Thank you to my friends and former producers Rick Delgado and Erik Nagel.

Thank you to my current producer, Keith Maresca, and my assistant, Angela Maresca, for your friendship and everything you do.

I want to thank the amazing staff at Compound Media.

I want to thank my friend Joe Currie for being there for the long haul since 1977.

Thanks to the hilarious celebrity comics who took the time to give me a blurb to endorse this book, including Andrew "Dice" Clay, Artie Lange, Joe Rogan, Lisa Lampanelli, and Colin Quinn.

I'd like to thank the very talented authors I worked with on this, Brad Trackman and Johnny Russo. I really enjoyed the process of doing this incredible thing of putting out a book. You two made it so easy and fun.

Thanks to my literary agent, Jill Marr, for getting us the deal.

Lastly, to everyone who purchased this book, thank you. I appreciate all my listeners who have stuck with me throughout the years.

CO-AUTHOR BIOS

JOHNNY RUSSO

Writer, comedian, and political analyst Johnny Russo began his career as a teenager on the comedy club stages of New York and eventually landed in another form of entertainment: politics. Johnny is a veteran writer, has been an operative on several presidential campaigns, and can be seen regularly on Fox News, C-SPAN, One America News and the Freeform channel, providing comedic political commentary.

BRAD TRACKMAN

Brad Trackman is a nationally touring headliner comedian with numerous television appearances. He has appeared most recently on CBS's The Late Late Show, CBS's Comics Unleashed, and AXS TV's Gotham Comedy Live. Brad started stand up in NYC, being a weekend regular at the Comedy Cellar, Gotham Comedy Club, Carolines on Broadway, Comic Strip Live, Broadway Comedy Club and Stand Up NY. Brad performs throughout the United States, Canada and parts of Europe. He resides in New Jersey with his wife Christina and son Tyler.